THE LIFE

A PORTRAIT OF JESUS

THE LIFE

A Portrait of Jesus

J. JOHN
and
CHRIS WALLEY

Authentic

ACKNOWLEDGEMENTS

We would like to thank Dr Tom Wright, Dr Mark Stibbe and Brian Draper for their comments on the first draft of this manuscript; your discernment, knowledge and scholarship were invaluable. We also want to express our thanks to Katharine Draper, Karen Minashi and Phillip Herbert for perceptive comments.

CONTENTS

INTRODUCTION

We live in hard times for heroes. There is a cynicism in our culture that eats away at even the most glorious reputations. Almost overnight, selfless geniuses turn out to be selfish fools, great leaders are revealed as insecure bullies and champions of morality are exposed as hypocrites. One of the few figures to survive with their reputation intact is Jesus Christ.

We cannot ignore Jesus. Consider the following:

- About one-third of the world's population consider themselves to be Christian, seek to follow Jesus and worship him as God. To Muslims – another twenty per cent – Jesus is a great prophet.
- The ethical code introduced by Jesus and his followers is the basis of much of the world's thinking. Throughout the Western world, and often beyond, it is the teachings of Jesus that underlie the legal and political systems.

- Western culture is still based upon Jesus. Whether obvious or concealed, the influence of Jesus and his followers in art, music, philosophy and literature is enormous. It is hard to understand Western culture unless you understand something of Jesus.

- Jesus' words have worked their way into the English language. Whenever we talk about 'a prodigal son', 'turning the other cheek', 'not casting stones', 'being a good Samaritan', we echo the words and images used by Jesus.

- Christianity is a global faith that transcends culture and language. In every inhabited continent, hundreds of millions of people are followers of Jesus.

- Jesus' teaching has proved to be durable. In the last two thousand years most of the world's great powers, empires and ideologies have at some time opposed what he stood for. Yet whether the opposition has been first-century Rome or twentieth-century communism the result has been the same. There has been a struggle; and when the dust settles, you find the empire is gone and Jesus' teachings – and his followers – remain.

- Millions of people from every culture, race and background claim that turning to Jesus has transformed their lives.

Clearly, whatever background we come from, Jesus deserves our attention. Yet there are a vast number of different understandings of who Jesus is and what he means. We live in an age when some people will believe almost everything with no evidence and others believe almost nothing in the face of overwhelming evidence. Jesus has received the attention of both. So there are those who will confidently say that Jesus was an alien, an Egyptian prince or an Indian mystic and there are those who will say – with equal confidence – that we can know almost nothing whatever about him. The combination of all these views has produced such a confusion that many people are now totally bewildered about who Jesus is.

We have written this book to try to help explain who Jesus is. But let us first say where we are coming from. Today's views about Jesus fall into three groups. A first group of people adopt what we might call the 'traditional' or 'mainstream' view of Jesus. This view, which has been held by almost all Christians of all denominations through the ages and is held by the vast majority of Christians today, is that Jesus was both man and God, that he rose from the dead and that he is still alive today. Those who hold to this view consider the Bible is a trustworthy record of who Jesus was, what he did and what he said.

A second group hold to what we can call the 'sceptical' view of Jesus. They reject the miraculous elements of the gospels and believe in a purely human Jesus: a wandering Jewish teacher who, after his death, somehow became viewed as the Son of God and Saviour. While they may be respectful of Jesus ('a wonderful teacher', 'the best man who ever lived') there is a vast gap between this Jesus and that of traditional Christianity. With this sceptical view of Jesus as a human and fallible figure comes a similar view of the records about him: the Bible's accounts are flawed and unreliable documents.

A third group believe in what we can call a 'New Age' Jesus. Their Jesus is some mystical figure, a guru or shaman, who was in touch with the spiritual world and whose closest parallels are with spiritual masters of the Eastern religions. Such people do not question the gospel accounts of Jesus' life but prefer to add to them or reinterpret them. And while those who believe in a 'New Age' Jesus treat him with honour, the Jesus they respect is merely one of many spiritual masters and is therefore very different from the unique figure of traditional, mainstream Christianity.

And where do we stand? We write this book from within the traditional, mainstream view of Jesus that has been held for twenty centuries. Yet having said this we want to qualify our position.

Firstly, our commitment to 'tradition' extends only to our views of who Jesus was and is. We are not 'traditionalists' in the sense that we automatically endorse anything the Christian church does as long as it's always been done that way. Even Jesus himself was critical of tradition. Not all traditions are good and we think that there are areas where the church has not done a very good job of reflecting its founder's teachings.

Secondly, having a traditional view of Jesus is not the same as having a cosy and comfortable Jesus. The real, authentic Jesus is a rather unsettling figure who both comforts those who are troubled and troubles those who are comfortable. In fact, the traditional Jesus is actually much more radical and challenging than any of the alternatives that have been constructed.

Thirdly, in taking such a view of Jesus, we are not saying 'just believe'. We acknowledge the existence of the alternative views on Jesus and engage with them throughout this book. In fact, one reason for writing this book is that we believe only the traditional view of Jesus makes sense and fits all the data about him.

ABOUT THIS BOOK

This book is written both for those who would claim to have faith in Jesus but who would like to know more about him and for those who are 'just looking'.

The book has two aims. First, it is a *guide* to who Jesus was, what he said, what he did and what he means for people today. Second, it is intended as *a defence* of the Jesus of the gospels. In the face of the alternative views of Jesus that exist today, it is a restatement of the traditional, mainstream view of who he was.

ABOUT US

We come from different backgrounds. J. John comes from a Greek Cypriot background. He has an MA in Theology, is a speaker and teacher based at St Andrew's in Chorleywood, Hertfordshire, and is a Canon of Coventry Cathedral (Church of England). J. John is married to Killy and they have three sons: Michael, Simeon and Benjamin. J. John grew up speaking the modern version of the Greek in which the New Testament was written. Chris Walley has a PhD in Geology and was an academic and consultant geologist for over twenty years; during this time he spent a total of eight years in Lebanon, where many aspects of culture and society were – and still are – much closer to the world of the gospels than those of modern Britain. He now lives in Swansea, where he is a writer. Chris is married to Alison and they have two sons, John and Mark. Chris is a member of a Baptist church. And both of us are Christians who have lived (and sometimes struggled) with who Jesus is and what he wants of us for a combined total of over fifty years.

SOME WORDS ON WORDS

We have deliberately chosen to use ordinary language. There is a good precedent for this: the gospels and the New Testament letters that describe what Jesus did are written in the everyday, ordinary Greek of the market place rather than the language of the scholars and philosophers.

Where we have quoted from the Bible we have used the New Living Translation. In order not to break up the flow of the text, we have put the Bible references for each chapter at the end of the book.

A few specific notes:

- Jesus is a personal name (Hebrew *Yeshua*, Greek *Iesus*) and 'Christ' ('Messiah') is a title. So 'Jesus Christ' is a contraction of 'Jesus the Christ'. However, most Christians use the names 'Jesus' and 'Christ' interchangeably. We have used 'Jesus'.

- Almost all the action of the gospels takes place in a small strip of land between the Mediterranean and the Jordan valley for which we use the geographic term 'Palestine'. 'Israel' or 'the nation of Israel' refers here, as it does in the New Testament, to God's people, rather than a place: in Jesus' day the Kingdom of Israel had long ceased to exist. Palestine consisted of three subdivisions at the time of the gospels: Galilee in the north, Samaria in the middle and Judea, which included the hills around Jerusalem, in the south. There was also a small area inhabited by Jews in Perea, just east of the Jordan.

- We have continued to use the term 'Old Testament' but it needs to be remembered that to Jesus and his contemporaries it wasn't the *Old* Testament at all; it was their Bible. On that note, we have used 'the Bible' and 'the Scriptures' as interchangeable terms.

- When writing about Jesus' period of teaching and healing there seems to be no alternative but to talk about his *ministry*. It's now an odd phrase in English but it has – or should have – overtones of service (as in 'ministering') which are helpful.

- Jesus called to him twelve *disciples* (disciple means 'learner'). After the resurrection these – with the exception of Judas – became the *apostles* (literally 'those who are sent').

- *Divine* is a useful adjective for anything to do with God. So to say that 'Jesus is divine' is not just another way of saying 'Jesus is excellent': it means that he is God.

LAYOUT

This book is divided into two. Chapters 1–4 look at issues to do with Jesus, such as what data we have, whether we can trust the gospels, and the political and religious background to the gospels. Chapters 5–15 deal with the life of Jesus from his birth onwards. Although these chapters are chronological, there are four chapters (8–11) which consider the topics: Jesus' followers, his miracles and how and what he taught.

Such a layout is unavoidable but we are conscious that some people will prefer to start with Jesus. We sympathize; so if you want to jump to Chapter 5 and then come back to the earlier chapters, then do so.

In addition to the normal text in the chapters, you will also find

! SECTIONS MARKED LIKE THIS

These sections are where we have taken time out from the main flow of the chapter to look at some particular issue.

WHAT DO WE KNOW ABOUT JESUS?

It would be easy to start this book on Jesus by telling the story of his life. Yet if we did that, quoting Bible passages on the way, some legitimate questions would arise:

- How do we know the Jesus story isn't a myth?
- Why is the Jesus of traditional Christianity the true one, when others believe in a very different Jesus?
- Aren't there other sources of information on Jesus?

So let's consider the data on Jesus.

THE GOSPELS

What we learn about the life of Jesus in the Bible we learn from the four gospels. Although the idea that Jesus is 'Saviour' and 'Lord' is present on every page of the rest of the New Testament, it is only in the four gospels that we get any details about Jesus' earthly life and ministry. The gospels are like four portraits of Jesus, each done in a different style and each showing him from a different angle.

The first three gospels, Matthew, Mark and Luke, have much in common and are often referred to as the *synoptic* (meaning that they can 'be seen side by side') gospels. Yet each of the three has its own characteristics:

- *Matthew's* Gospel has a strong Jewish flavour and contains many references to Jewish beliefs and practices. A key theme in Matthew's Gospel is how Jesus fulfils Old Testament prophecy. Jesus is shown as being the Son of David and the Messiah, the long promised king. Jesus is also a great teacher, in the line of Moses, who teaches and explains the new Law (the *Torah*) to his followers. Matthew also shows how, through Jesus, God's plan for the whole world will be fulfilled.

- In *Mark*, the shortest of the gospels, Jesus is portrayed as the Son of God, a dynamic, authoritative figure who is constantly on the move. Mark says a lot about Jesus' actions, his power over the natural and supernatural world, and his death.

- *Luke's* Gospel is unique in that it has a sequel, the book of Acts, and is therefore part of a two-volume work. Luke emphasizes Jesus as the saviour and rescuer sent by God. Luke has a particular interest in those whom we would today call 'the marginalized': women, children, the poor and those rejected by society.

John, the fourth gospel, is different in style. In John's Gospel, Jesus is presented as the one who, by his words and actions, reveals who God is. Seven great statements in which he says 'I am' highlight the claims of Jesus. In these he claims to be 'the bread of life', 'the light of the world', 'the gate', 'the good shepherd', 'the resurrection and the life', 'the way, the truth and the life', and the 'true vine'. Although some sceptical scholars have considered that John's Gospel is a less reliable source of information on Jesus than the synoptics, there is no evidence for this. John's sequence of events makes sense and his knowledge of the landscape of Palestine is accurate. Frequently, too, there are details in John (such as who ran faster to the tomb on the first Easter morning[1] and the number of fish caught[2]) that seem to be eyewitness touches.

Who wrote the gospels and when?

Early church tradition considered Matthew, one of Jesus' disciples, to be the author of the first gospel and Mark and Luke, two men who were involved in the church in its very first years, to have authored the second and third gospels. John, another disciple, was believed to have written the fourth gospel. There seems no reason why these traditions shouldn't be correct. In this case, two authors were eyewitnesses to the events they describe while the other authors must have used sources: eye-witness accounts, traditions and other records. Given the strong likenesses between many passages in the first three gospels there is agreement that they shared at least one common source, but there is far less agreement about what this source was and how it was used. The whole subject of how the gospels came together is so complex that it is not treated here; there are many books that cover this in detail (see *For Further Reading* at the end of this book).

But when were the gospels written? Archaeological evidence suggests that John's Gospel was in circulation soon after AD 100. In fact, most scholars believe that all the gospels were written earlier and there is evidence for all the synoptic gospels being written before AD 65. So, for instance, Acts, the second of Luke's two volumes, ends with eight chapters on the legal proceedings to do with Paul, concluding, on the final page, with Paul still awaiting trial in Rome in AD 62–64. For a skilled author like Luke, such a cliffhanger of an ending is odd. The most obvious explanation is that this was when Luke was writing and Paul's trial still lay in the future. In fact, Luke and Acts might be part of the defence brief for Paul's appeal.

Another line of evidence centres on the appalling events that took place in Jerusalem in AD 70. Forty years after the death of Jesus, the simmering tensions between Jews and Romans boiled over, a revolt erupted and Jerusalem was besieged and mercilessly destroyed. The loss of the temple, God's dwelling place on earth, shook the Jewish faith to its core. Yet although the synoptic gospels record prophecies by Jesus that the temple would be destroyed, there is not the slightest hint that this had already occurred.

The idea that Matthew, Mark and Luke were written by the middle of the 60s makes a lot of sense. By then the effects of age and persecution would have been beginning to thin out the disciples of Jesus; Peter, for example, is thought to have been executed in AD 65. With rapidly expanding churches and the beginnings of heretical movements, there would have been a strong demand for an authoritative, written record of what Jesus had said and done.

OTHER NEW TESTAMENT DOCUMENTS

As well as the four gospels, the New Testament also contains the book of Acts, the letters and Revelation.

What we learn in Acts is how the very first Christians understood Jesus. This comes over most clearly in the summaries of what the apostles taught about Jesus. They made Jesus central to their teaching and portrayed him as more than a man: he was the Messiah, the 'author of life' and the one who would come to judge all people at the end of time. Above all, Acts presents Jesus as being risen from the dead and, through his Spirit, present with his followers.

The letters are important as evidence about Jesus, not so much because they tell us a lot about his life, but because most of them are earlier than the gospels. So, for instance, it is generally agreed that the letters to the Galatians and the Thessalonians were written in AD 48–51: within twenty years of the crucifixion. Yet interestingly enough even these early letters talk about Jesus as 'the Lord', the unique mediator between humankind and God, the one who has been raised from the dead and the one who will return in judgement.

JESUS OUTSIDE THE NEW TESTAMENT

Not that long ago defenders of Christianity used to make a great deal about the evidence for Jesus outside the Bible. The reason for this was that there were people who denied that a historical Jesus had ever existed and who believed he was a totally mythical or legendary creation. Against this argument, the evidence from such writers as Tacitus and Josephus was valuable.

But the debate has moved on and now it is very rare to meet anyone who has done any serious study on the subject who is prepared to say that Jesus never lived. Although sceptical scholars may consider Jesus no more than a purely human preacher, they do recognize his existence. Indeed, it is surprising how much historical accuracy scholars are now prepared to credit to the gospels. For instance, in 2001 the BBC showed a major documentary series on Jesus entitled *Son of God*, which listed over twenty academic consultants, many of whom were not Christians (a number were Jewish). What surprised many people was the sheer amount of the gospel accounts that they were prepared to treat as historical fact. The programme was described as offering 'firm evidence for the existence of Jesus, perhaps the best attested life in the ancient world.' In saying this, the BBC was not going out on a limb: the existence of some sort of historical Jesus is now taken for granted amongst scholars who have studied first-century Palestine. So much of the gospels has been shown to fit the cultural, archaeological and historical data that to dismiss them as entirely fiction is now acknowledged as a ridiculous position.

Because of this, the witness of authors who were not Christians to the existence of Jesus has less impact than it did. But it is a witness that is still worth a brief mention.

Roman authors

In his life, Jesus was an insignificant character in a minor province of the Roman Empire. So it is not surprising that there is little in the historical records about him. In fact, documentation on most figures of the time is poor. For instance, outside the gospel accounts, what we know about Pontius Pilate, the governor of the Province of Judea for eleven years, would fit on the back of a postcard.

Works have survived from various Roman authors that mention, in passing, the spread of the 'Jesus cult' in the first century, but they tell us little that we do not know from the letters of the New Testament. There were apparently 'Christians' in Rome by the mid-40s and riots among the Jews over the preaching of Jesus as the Christ in AD 49. Tacitus, writing around AD 115 about the fire of Rome fifty years earlier, says this about Christians: 'The founder of this sect, Christus, was given the death penalty in the reign of Tiberius by the procurator Pontius Pilate; suppressed for the moment, the detestable superstition broke out again, not only in Judea where the evil originated, but also in the city [of Rome] to which everything horrible and shameful flows and where it grows.'

At about the same time, Pliny the Younger wrote from what is now Turkey to the Emperor Trajan for a ruling on whether to execute these Christians who 'worshipped Christ as a god'.

One longer account is by the writer Josephus (AD 37–100), whose books are a vital resource for events in first-century Palestine. Josephus fought against the Romans in the Jewish revolt of AD 66–70 before switching sides and ended up in Rome as an expert on Jewish affairs. In one of his books, *The Antiquities of the Jews* (written around AD 95), Josephus refers to Jesus:

> Now, there was about this time Jesus, a wise man, if it be lawful to call him a man, for he was a doer of surprising works, a teacher of such men as receive the truth with pleasure. He

drew over to him both many of the Jews, and many of the Greeks. He was the Messiah. And when Pilate, at the suggestion of the principal men among us, had condemned him to the cross, those that loved him at the first did not forsake him; for he appeared to them alive again the third day, as the divine prophets had foretold these and ten thousand other wonderful things concerning him. And the tribe of Christians, so named for him, are not extinct to this day.[3]

Although the authenticity of this passage has been challenged, most scholars now believe that the main parts at least are genuine.*

While none of these accounts says a great deal about Jesus, they do confirm that he existed, that he lived in Palestine, that he was considered to be the Messiah and that he was executed under Pontius Pilate who governed Palestine from AD 26 to 36.

The Dead Sea Scrolls

In 1947 a collection of ancient manuscripts was found in a series of caves in the area west of the Dead Sea and they have

---

* At the very least, Josephus wrote that Jesus had been a good man, had done wonders, had accumulated followers from within Judaism and outside it and, after accusations from the Jewish leaders, had been crucified by Pilate.

since been slowly translated and published. Despite periodic claims to the contrary, the scrolls make no mention of Jesus and appear to have been largely written before his ministry began. The scrolls are, however, useful in that they give an insight into the Jewish mindset of the times. Before the discovery of the scrolls, much of our knowledge of Judaism came from considerably later sources and it was not always clear how Jesus and his followers related to the Jewish faith. The Dead Sea Scrolls have shown us that the Jewish faith in early first-century Palestine was much more varied than had been assumed, and many of Jesus' views and sayings now fit much better into the Jewish world of his time.

The apocryphal books of the New Testament

In recent years there has been much interest in what are called the 'apocryphal'* books of the New Testament. The apocryphal books are those documents that circulated within the early church but which were excluded when the formal list of approved books of the New Testament was drawn up well before the end of the second century. These apocryphal books include stories, letters, teaching manuals and visions.

---

* The word *apocryphal* originally meant 'hidden' but came to mean 'unapproved' or 'of dubious authenticity'. Just to make life complex there is an Old Testament Apocrypha too.

In the last hundred years or so, some scholars have looked again at these documents in the hope that they will yield more information about Jesus than we have in the existing gospels.* Yet no one has made a convincing case for any of these adding anything significant to what the existing four gospels say.

* * *

Where does this leave us? The answer is that we are much where we always were. We have the hard data from the four gospels and little else. From Josephus, Tacitus and the others we glimpse a faint silhouette of Jesus. But only in the gospels do we have anything like a full picture of who Jesus was and what he said and did.

Yet the limited data that we have is important. The sceptical option of treating Jesus as a myth has vanished. To hold such a view always required an extraordinary faith that somehow people could make up the whole thing. And equally, if these facts remove the sceptic's option to dismiss Jesus entirely, they also limit the freedom of those with New Age

---

* There has been particular interest in the Gospel of Thomas, a mere 114 verses of isolated and rather random sayings attributed to Jesus. 'Thomas', however, is now felt to be a very late second-century document and it adds little to what we know of Jesus from the exisiting gospels.

sympathies to reinvent Jesus in a way that fits better with their own views. The Jesus of the Bible firmly belongs to a time and a place; he is a Jew of early first-century Palestine and our views of who he was – and is – have to take that into account.

CAN WE TRUST THE GOSPELS?

The issue of the reliability of the gospels is an important one and it is obviously relevant to anyone who is exploring the truth of Christianity. The Jesus that traditional Christianity proclaims is a figure who demands total loyalty. You can hardly make that sort of commitment to someone who is a fantasy figure.

So are the gospels trustworthy? There are two main issues here and both need looking at. To understand what they are, let's think of something that may seem a long way from the gospels. Imagine that you are looking through the effects of your recently deceased grandfather. Suddenly, among his papers, you find a few pages of writing in which he appears to describe how, during the D-Day landings, he fought heroically in an appalling battle in France. Before sending a copy to the local regimental museum for their files, you would ask two questions. The first would be, quite simply, was this document ever meant to be *history*? Was it intended as a factual account of real events or was it something else? Was it perhaps a scrap from some uncompleted novel? Might it be a parable or an allegory, something intended to make a point through fiction? After all, Spielberg's film *Saving Private Ryan*, which is set in the same time and place, is, for all its realism, a work of fiction. It is not historical fact.

If you decided that your grandfather had intended his writing to be treated as history, a second question would arise. Was it *reliable* history? Now a new set of questions arises. Did your grandfather really fight in the events he described? How accurate was his memory? Was his account based on notes he made shortly afterwards or was it written in old age, when his memory had begun to fade?

These two big and basic questions can be asked of the gospels. Are they *history*? Are they *reliable history*?

ARE THE GOSPELS HISTORY?

The best indication of a document's purpose is what the author says about it. So if an author prefaces a book with the words 'This is a fairy tale I told my children' we know that we are dealing with fiction.

Fortunately, we have just that kind of statement of intent at the start of Luke's Gospel:

Most honourable Theophilus:
Many people have written accounts about the events that took place among us. They used as their source material the reports

circulating among us from the early disciples and other eye-witnesses of what God has done in fulfilment of his promises. Having carefully investigated all of these accounts from the beginning, I have decided to write a careful summary for you, to reassure you of the truth of all you were taught.[1]

Luke makes two claims. The first is that his document is a truthful historical account. The second is that he has carefully consulted eyewitnesses and looked at earlier reports in order to ensure that's what it is.

But are the gospels *just* histories? Are they neutral, purely factual accounts written by people who have no interest other than retelling just what happened? The answer is that they are not. Towards the end of his gospel, John writes: 'Jesus' disciples saw him do many other miraculous signs besides the ones recorded in this book. But these are written so that you may believe that Jesus is the Messiah, the Son of God, and that by believing in him you will have life.'[2] The purpose of the gospel-writers in writing what they did was not just to inform; it was also to convince.

Now the existence of such a purpose in the writing of the gospels should not surprise or unsettle us. Even today most histories and biographies are written from some sort of conviction, even if it is no more than a belief that their subject should interest us. Otherwise why bother? And the fact that someone has a reason for writing something does not necessarily compromise its historical value. There would be no contradiction between your grandfather writing an account of D-Day with the purpose of showing the horror of war and him writing it accurately. In fact, any lies or exaggerations would, if detected, weaken his argument.

The gospels, then, are history; but it is history told by authors with strong convictions.

ARE THE GOSPELS RELIABLE HISTORY?

The question of whether the gospels are reliable raises a whole host of issues that can be summarized under four headings: techniques, translation, transmission and texts.

Techniques

Modern authors use a vast range of tools and techniques in writing. So, for instance, we can use quotation marks to show we are reporting speech or to show that a word is being used in a way that is not strictly literal. We have punctuation marks such as brackets, full stops, commas and italics to clarify exactly what we mean and to show where we are placing our emphasis. Ancient writers had none of these tools, so we sometimes have to guess exactly how to translate the original text into modern English.

Translation

Although Jesus may have known Greek, the language he taught in was Aramaic, a linguistic cousin of Hebrew. As the gospels were written in Greek, what he said has therefore been translated. Now, as anyone who has ever tried to translate anything knows, transferring ideas from one language to another is difficult. To take the most basic of examples: how do you translate the French *Bonjour* into English? 'Good day'? No, that's far too formal. 'Good morning' or 'Good afternoon'? Perhaps, but not always. 'Hi', maybe? It's not easy, is it? In fact, a perfect translation is difficult. The reality is that in any translation you inevitably end up doing some rephrasing. The gospels are no different and what we have in them is probably best described as an accurate paraphrase of what Jesus said.

Because most of us do not read the gospels in the original Greek, a further translation – into English – has occurred. Yet although these issues of translation may seem major, their significance should not be overstated. For one thing, the message of Jesus occurs in four gospels and comparing them can often clear up any question over what one passage means. For another, Christianity is not about understanding complex philosophical issues that require that we understand precise shades of meaning. Christianity is the presentation of a person, Jesus Christ, and that is something that can easily survive translation.

Transmission

Anyone thinking about the accuracy of the gospels must recognize the fact that there is a time gap between the events they describe taking place and the accounts being written down. In the case of the synoptic gospels, this time gap is around thirty years; with John, it is perhaps fifty years. That may seem a long time but several things need to be said.

First, there must have been earlier stages in the gospels. Indeed, Luke mentions in the preface to his gospel the existence of source documents. For all we know, some of these documents may have been written down shortly after the events themselves.

Second, and probably more significantly, we must not overlook the role of memorization in the culture in which the gospels were written. In our world, we are never far from pen and paper and have little need to acquire this skill. But in those days, much of learning depended on memorization.

In fact, it is easy enough to imagine teaching situations (rather similar to those which still operate in many settings in the Middle East) where a leader would recite line by line what Jesus said, or did, to rows of students and they would repeat it word for word until they were letter-perfect. Many of Jesus' teachings are in the form of parables, proverbs or structured sayings that are ideally suited for memorization.

A third factor is that the early church grew up in a setting where there was a long tradition of giving God's words extraordinary reverence. Scribes who copied and re-copied Old Testament documents went to remarkable lengths to make sure they did not add to or take away from the original. They cross-checked manuscripts for accuracy by counting words in methods whose closest parallels today occur in the checking of computer code. All the evidence suggests that Jesus' followers treated what he said with a similar respect. So transmission may present less of a problem than we think.

Texts

A fourth issue that needs to be considered when we think of reliability is that of texts. All we have considered so far is how the text of the gospel was written down in the middle of the first century. We need to get from there to the present day, from the original handwritten scrolls to today's Bible. Can this gap too be bridged?

Here there is a considerable basis for confidence. The Dead Sea Scrolls have shown that Old Testament documents were copied with the greatest of care and the New Testament documents would, no doubt, have been similarly treated. Over five thousand manuscripts of the Greek New Testament, varying in size from a few verses to entire books, are known from the second to sixteenth centuries. From the end of the second century there are also many copies of Latin translations of the New Testament.

In summary, there is reason to believe that the message of Jesus has been transmitted accurately. But this is not something that we have to take as a matter of faith: the accuracy can be tested. Where the New Testament can be checked against outside sources its reliability can often be confirmed. For example, consider the formal title of Pontius Pilate. In what we might call the Roman Colonial Service of the first century, titles changed with a bewildering rapidity and it is easy to get confused. Tacitus and Josephus, writing at the end of the first century, both refer to Pilate as a 'procurator', a term for a civilian ruling official. The New Testament avoids that term and simply uses a word meaning 'governor' which may cover both a military and civilian leadership. Now what is interesting is that both Tacitus and Josephus seem to have made a mistake because in Pilate's time the rulers of Judea were military governors or prefects; they became procurators only later during the reign of Claudius. An inscription found in 1961 confirms that Pilate was indeed not a procurator but a prefect. It's a trivial point but it's interesting that the gospel writers dodge a trap that two of the best non-Christian authorities fall into.

There are many other things like this. On matters where they can be tested by history or archaeology, the gospel authors seem to be careful and cautious writers.

* * *

The gospels claim to be history and there is nothing to argue that they are not just that. But are they accurate, reliable history? We would argue that they are. True, the gospels do not follow all the practices of our modern histories or biographies. However, to make demands that *our* standards must be met is a kind of cultural arrogance: we are saying, in effect, 'Either you write our way or we will not treat you seriously!' What we have in the gospels are documents that claim to be an accurate and reliable history: they demand to be taken very seriously.

HOW ARE WE TO APPROACH THE GOSPELS?

In this book we will spend time looking at the gospels. The issue of how we approach the gospels - and the Bible - is not simple. After all, most Christians do not believe the gospels because of the archaeological or historical evidence; they believe them because they have put their faith in the Jesus whom they find in the gospels. In other words, a faith in Jesus often occurs *before* a trust in the Bible. And the archaeological or historical evidence is, at best, merely supporting evidence.

There are two opposing ways of looking at the gospels. The first is to adopt an attitude of *disbelief*. Here, the New Testament documents are viewed as fictional or mythical to such an extent that they can be ignored. Those who hold to this sort of disbelief often portray the situation as being one where the Christian has 'blind faith' and the sceptic doesn't. '*You* have faith,' they say, 'I don't.' Of course, it isn't that simple. Their disbelief is, in fact, as much faith as our Christian belief.

It is always worthwhile gently probing the origins of such scepticism. While such views of the reliability of the gospels can be held because of intense and learned studies of the New

Testament documents, they generally aren't. Often, this sort of disbelief turns out to be based on something 'I saw on the television' or 'I read in a paper'. Such views need to be challenged. And it also has to be said that sometimes such a disbelief may be held for other motives. Jesus is a challenging figure who makes demands on our lives and sometimes the most convenient response is to treat him as fictional. Disbelief, as well as belief, can be the result of wishful thinking.

The second attitude to the gospels is that of *trust*. In this view, these documents are not just a book, they are *God's* book. They are trustworthy because they are what he has spoken. Most Christians would hold such an attitude for three reasons.

Firstly, when you accept that God is part of the equation, the whole basis of how you look at the trustworthiness of the New Testament changes. Once you allow for a God who controls and manages all things, the idea that a book might contain his message to the human race seems perfectly possible. Indeed, if you have come to believe that in Jesus, God was making a unique and costly intervention in the affairs of the human race, the idea that he left a reliable record of that event seems entirely logical.

Secondly, those who have put their faith in Jesus come to know something of the testimony of the Holy Spirit to the truth of God's word. This is one of those internal and subjective experiences that those who are outside the faith find frustrating. But the fact is that Christians from all ages and cultures have reported the same thing: once they came to believe in Jesus, the Bible gained a new sense of authority. The wording they use varies – 'I found Jesus in it', 'the Bible came alive' – but the underlying experience is the same.

Thirdly – and perhaps most importantly – beginning to know and trust God makes a real difference to how you view the whole issue of the trustworthiness of the Bible. Imagine you begin a long correspondence with someone you have never met, and then get to know them personally. Before you met them, you could only evaluate their letters on the evidence of what they contained. You read the text and asked yourself whether it sounded convincing. Did what they say match the facts? But once you came to know the writer, things changed; you now trusted the letters because you knew the one who wrote them. The same happens when someone comes to faith in Jesus: the basis of their confidence now shifts from being based entirely on the evidence of archaeology or history to the nature of God himself. Jesus is trustworthy, so the documents that talk about him are trustworthy.

Yet these twin attitudes of disbelief and trust raise a problem: what position is someone to take who is 'enquiring', perhaps reading the gospels for the very first time? It is hardly fair to say 'just trust' to someone who knows nothing of the Jesus who is the basis of the trust that Christians have in the Bible. What attitude are they to hold? The best answer is to suggest that such a person adopt a position of what we might call *provisional trust*. This is the attitude that we have in most situations when we meet someone for the first time. We say to ourselves something like this: 'For the moment, I trust you. I give you a chance to prove yourself. But my decision is not yet final and permanent.' Eventually, of course, you will decide whether someone is – or isn't – trustworthy, but meanwhile you give them the benefit of the doubt. To take such a view towards the gospels is to adopt an open-minded attitude that you are prepared, *for the moment*, to accept that they are reliable and trustworthy.

If you are seeking, we would urge that you adopt this attitude. Read the gospels with an open mind and be prepared to be challenged. And at some point you may find that your provisional trust is turning into something much more solid.

THE RELIGIOUS BACKGROUND

To understand who Jesus was and what he taught, we must understand something of the Jewish faith and the religious traditions of his time. In thinking about what we might call 'the religious dimension' of Jesus' world we come to something that many people today find alien. In the contemporary West, even those people who consider themselves to be religious generally wear their religion lightly. Today, a religious faith is an accessory to our life, not an essential part of it. The result is that it is easy, even for those people who count themselves as religious, to spend most of a day without doing any activity that is religious or even thinking any 'religious' thoughts. While there were such people in Jesus' day they would have been the exception. Religion, for Jews at least, was something that shaped everything you were, you did and you said. Your faith wasn't an add-on to your life, it was the foundation and framework around which you built your life.

When we try to find out exactly what it was like to be a Jew in Jesus' day, we find ourselves faced with much that is uncertain. Nevertheless, we can think of being Jewish as having two aspects: having a history and holding to certain beliefs and practices.

THE HISTORY

The history of the Jewish people shaped their identity and, moreover, gave them hope in even the darkest of days. The Jewish people in Jesus' day did not see themselves as just one more religious or racial group in the world. They saw themselves as special, as God's own people and central to God's purposes in the world. They were not just a by-product of history: they were the focus of history. This sense of destiny underlies every page in the gospels. It also explains why, by Jesus' day, the Jewish people were frustrated with the way things had turned out. For the Christian, the history of the Jewish people until the time of Jesus is important: it is our history too.

That history started with Adam and Eve, the first humans. Having been placed in the Garden of Eden, Adam and Eve had lost God's blessing by disobedience and had been expelled into a world of evil and suffering. Ever since, human existence had been a long way from what it was meant to be. Centuries later, God had begun to restore the human race by choosing Abraham as the father of a people through whom blessing would return to the world.

God made promises to Abraham as part of a *covenant*, the most binding and unbreakable of agreements. In this covenant God promised Abraham that he would bless and protect his descendants for ever; that he would make them a great nation, give them a land of their own and bless all the peoples of the world through them. Over the next few generations, God's promises began to take shape and soon Abraham's descendants had multiplied to twelve tribes.

Yet several hundred years after Abraham, things went wrong and God's people found themselves enslaved in Egypt. God, however, spectacularly rescued them and, in the events called 'the Exodus', led them out of Egypt under the leadership of Moses. In the wilderness, God revealed the nature of the covenant more fully to Moses. He increased his promises of blessing but also communicated more fully what it meant to be one of God's covenant people. If the people were to enjoy the covenant's blessings then they had to have complete loyalty to God, had to worship him alone and had to obey the rules he gave. These rules were laid out in the Law (the *Torah* in Hebrew; what we call the Old Testament) and the Ten Commandments are a summary of these requirements. The purpose of these laws was to ensure that God's people would be special. They were to be distinctly different from the nations – the Gentiles – around them: they were to be *holy*. A sign of that holiness for men was circumcision, which came to define what it was to be Jewish.

At the heart of the covenant was the exclusive privilege the Jewish people had of knowing God. Symbolic of this was the way that God had revealed his name to his people so that they could know him as 'Yahweh'.* This name of God, which occurs over six thousand times in the Old Testament, is translated in English Bibles as 'the LORD'. Yet in reality, the relationship between the Jewish people ('Israel') and Yahweh was far from smooth and its highs and lows form the great storyline of the Old Testament.

Eventually, after a forty-year period in the wilderness because of disobedience, the Jewish people gained control of most of the territory God had promised them. The greatest extent of their kingdom was reached around 1000 BC under the reign of King David. To David, the greatest of all the kings, God reaffirmed the covenant and added yet another promise: David was to have a glorious son and be the founder of an unending line of kings. The prophecy was partially fulfilled under Solomon, David's son, who built a majestic temple that came to be the focus of the Jewish religion.

The reigns of David and Solomon were the high water mark of Jewish history: God's king ruled in peace, justice and prosperity

---

* The name Yahweh came to be treated as so holy that ultimately it was never spoken aloud and was never fully written down. In fact the belief that 'Yahweh' is the correct pronunciation is something of a guess. An older English translation was 'Jehovah'.

over a Jewish people in a Jewish land. Yet the glory days were short-lived and things soon went tragically downhill. The kingdom split along tribal lines into northern and southern parts and the exclusive worship of Yahweh that was central to the covenant began to wane. The northern kingdom soon slipped into pagan practices and anarchy. In 722 BC the Assyrians conquered it, took much of its population away and relocated them in what is now the northern part of Iraq. The Assyrians resettled other conquered peoples in the area of the old northern kingdom; the result was the Samaritans, a people considered ever afterwards by most Jews to be religiously and racially suspect.

The southern kingdom, ruled by a line of kings descended from David and centred on the temple at Jerusalem, fared somewhat better. Yet eventually it too fell away from the worship of Yahweh and was conquered by the Babylonians in 586 BC. The temple was destroyed and many of the nation's leaders were taken into exile in Babylon (in the southern part of modern Iraq). Many others left the land to go to Egypt and other countries. In 539 BC the Persians conquered Babylon and the Jewish captives were allowed to return to their homeland. Significantly for the future, not all the Jews did. A sizeable Jewish population continued to exist outside Israel, where they became increasingly independent of how things were done 'back home'.

Despite the extraordinary deliverance from Babylon, things were never the same for the Jewish people after the exile. There was no return to independence and Gentile rule continued: the Babylonians were simply replaced as the conquering power by the Persians. There were no new kings and although the temple was rebuilt, it was only a partial success. There had been a certainty that God dwelt in Solomon's temple but the restored temple aroused no such confidence. Perhaps as a reaction, the Jewish religion began to shift away from being centred on temple worship to local meetings at what became termed 'the synagogue'. The great hope of God's king ruling in glory over Jewish people in their own land seemed a long way away.

By the time of Jesus' birth, hundreds of years later, matters were no better. A Jew looking around at the religious landscape then would have seen little that was encouraging. The rule and influence of the Gentiles now seemed to be unshakeable: the Greeks had replaced the Persians and had been replaced in turn by the Romans. True, King Herod was rebuilding the temple on a magnificent scale but he was a Roman puppet and only questionably Jewish. Of the three great offices of the Jewish faith – kings, prophets and priests – all had gone or become tainted. The kings had ended with the exile, prophecy had waned not long after the return (the last proper prophet was considered to be Malachi, who had spoken around 450 BC) and the priests were now political appointees approved by Rome.

Yet Jews still believed they were God's covenant people, and because the covenant was binding, they knew that God could be relied on: one day he would deliver them. Central to this hope was the return of the promised king, the Messiah, or, to use the Greek, 'the Christ', from the line of David. There were various ideas about the Messiah, but most Jews believed that when he came he would become king, defeat the enemies of God's people and bring justice, peace and holiness to Israel. Under the Messiah, Israel would be great and glorious and would bless the nations of the world. While people assumed the Messiah would be human, much of what was expected of him – an eternal rule, Godlike wisdom and awesome power – required that he be more than an ordinary human being.

! JESUS AND JUDAISM

There are two opposing errors regarding Jesus and the Jewish faith. One error has been to ignore Jesus' Jewish background and beliefs. So some people treat him as some sort of universal man whose Jewishness is irrelevant and even attribute to him beliefs, such as reincarnation, that no Jew would have held. The other error is to treat Jesus as no more than any other Jewish teacher or *rabbi* and no different from the other preachers who wandered around Palestine in those days.

The reality is that while Jesus was Jewish and taught much that fitted within Judaism, he claimed to be far more than just another teacher. As we shall see, he saw himself as being above all previous teachers and prophets, as the one who fulfilled all God's promises to Israel and as God come in person to his people.

We cannot – and must not – ignore the Jewishness of Jesus. But we must also be prepared to accept that he was much more than just another rabbi.

BELIEFS AND PRACTICES

In telling the history of the Jewish people, we mentioned some of the key beliefs and practices the Jews of Jesus' day held. If we are to understand the gospels, we need to know something more of the things that were central to the Jewish faith.

God

One of the most distinctive features of the Jewish faith was that it believed there was only one God. This God – Yahweh – was the one universal God, whose power and authority were unlimited. In an age when the Greeks and Romans believed in many gods, this Jewish insistence on one single and universal God was radical. It was also a source of confrontation, particularly with the Romans, who were beginning to suggest that their emperors were divine and deserved worship.

Yet for all their beliefs that there was only one God, the Jews of Jesus' day were exploring the issue of how this God related to the world he had made. God's Wisdom, God's Spirit and God's Word were all talked about in various ways as the means by which this invisible and all-powerful Yahweh could communicate who he was to the world. As these things were discussed there were hints – but no more – that the oneness of God might be more complex than it seemed. Nevertheless, in Jewish eyes the vast gap between God and the human race remained.

God's word

Yahweh was a God who had spoken to his covenant people. What he said was recorded in the Law, which was, quite literally, beyond value. The Law was treated as the sum of all wisdom and it was memorized, recited, guarded and debated. The depth of dedication Jews of Jesus' day had to God's word was enormous: it would have been normal for someone to have memorized entire books of the Old Testament.

God's temple

The temple in Jerusalem played a central role in the faith of most Jews of Jesus' day, especially those who lived in Palestine. Rebuilt in majestic splendour by Herod the Great, the temple was where sacrifices for sin were offered before a holy God. The temple was the spiritual centre of the world, the point where heaven and earth met and the place where God dwelt with his people.

Yet for all the temple's importance, there was a general awareness in Jesus' day that things were not right with it.

The temple administration was corrupt and the whole system had become a lucrative money machine involving dubious practices. Some Jews felt that the temple needed cleansing, others that it needed destroying. One of the hopes for the Messiah was that he would restore or renew the temple.

Ritual purity

An essential part of Jewish belief was the idea of 'ritual purity': that to please God you had to be pure, clean and uncontaminated before him. Although ritual purity is one of the most difficult concepts for most modern Westerners to understand, it cannot be ignored: there are a vast number of references to it in the gospels. In fact, the stunning abolition of the entire concept of ritual purity by the first Christians was one of the main factors that led to Christianity becoming separate from the Jewish faith.

Unless they come from a Jewish or Islamic background, people living in the modern West tend to think of purity and cleanliness simply in terms of hygiene. Yet in Jesus' culture, purity and 'being clean' were not concerned with hygiene and avoiding disease; they were about 'holiness'. In Jewish eyes, everything was either clean or unclean. In order to be ritually pure before God, you had to avoid contact with those things that were unclean and, if you did make contact with them, you had to undergo cleansing.

The Law gave definitions about what was unclean. You became unclean by doing certain things (such as committing adultery and incest), having contact with dead bodies, eating certain unclean animals, having certain skin ailments and so on. And to make matters worse, uncleanness was contagious: touching someone who was unclean made you unclean. While some uncleanness could be avoided (for instance, by keeping to a kosher diet), there were some situations (such as menstruation, childbirth and dealing with the dead) where becoming unclean was unavoidable. There was no blame attached to the unavoidable forms of uncleanness; it was just 'one of those things'. But however you became unclean, you had to be cleansed and there were approved rituals of cleansing in every case, many of which involved ceremonial washing.

The result of these laws – which extended into every area of life – was that people were continually reminded of the issue of holiness. To keep these rules of purity was to live a life that was separate and very distinct from that of the Gentiles. These rules of what was clean and unclean were like a series of concentric barriers around zones of increasing holiness. Outside them was all the uncleanness and impurity of the Gentile world; inside them was the purity of God's holy people. At the centre of these zones of purity was God's dwelling place, the temple. There a succession of courts, curtains and barriers created ever purer spaces so that finally, behind a curtain in the innermost part of the temple, God dwelt in his awesome purity. Only the priests, under conditions of extreme cleanliness, could enter into God's presence at the temple's heart.

The Sabbath

One day a week – Saturday – was kept as a holy day, the Sabbath. On that day, no work could be done and even non-work activities were restricted. The Sabbath was another way in which Jews showed that they were God's people. If the rules on purity emphasized that they were to have a special attitude to things, the rules about the Sabbath showed that they were also to have a special attitude to time.

Feasts

The Jewish calendar was marked by a number of major feasts. These were not simply a time for food and a family get-together; they were times that commemorated great events in Jewish history. Four main feasts are mentioned in the gospels:

- The *Feast of Passover* (or Pesach) occurred in March or April and celebrated the liberation of the Israelites from foreign slavery in Egypt in the events of the Exodus.
- The *Feast of Pentecost* (or Shavuot) came fifty days after Passover. Coinciding with the first grain harvest, it celebrated the giving of the Law.

- The *Feast of Tabernacles* (Sukkoth) occurred in October and commemorated the forty years the Israelites had spent in the desert.
- The *Feast of Dedication* (Hanukkah) occurred in late November or December and commemorated the cleansing of the temple in 165 BC during what became called the Maccabean Revolt.

All these feasts could only really be properly celebrated at the temple in Jerusalem. This was particularly true of Passover, which required the slaughtering of a sacrificial lamb. The feasts were a way of reminding people who they were, what they stood for and what they hoped for.

* * *

Any non-Jew who had contact with Jews at the time of Jesus, especially those in Palestine, would probably have found their faith irritating, baffling and intriguing. They would, no doubt, have been irritated by the Jewish exclusivity and their view that all Gentiles were unclean. The Jewish laws on purity, diet and the Sabbath would have baffled them. They would have been intrigued by the absence of idols and the simplicity (and logic) of having just one God, rather than the warring crowd of Greek and Roman gods and goddesses.

Yet in thinking about the Jewish faith of Jesus' day, we must not lose sight of the fact that there was, at its centre, a problem. Judaism was based on the idea of being a holy nation, of there being a Jewish land ruled with Jewish laws by a Jewish king. There was no concept of a religion-state divide. The kingdom the Jewish people hoped for was one where every aspect of life could be under God's holy rule.

That was the hope. The reality was very different.

POWERS, POLITICS AND PRESSURES

I n Jesus' day, the reality the Jews lived under was shaped by Greek culture and Roman power. Both were a threat.

GREEK CULTURE

History

The spread of Greek culture into Palestine was due to Alexander the Great (356–323 BC), who, by his death at the age of thirty-two, had created an empire that stretched from Greece to the borders of India. The vision of Alexander and his followers was not just for power and empire; it was for the spread of the Greek way of life. Wherever they conquered, Alexander's forces set up colonies and built cities that were outposts of Greece. And although Alexander's empire did not long survive his death, his vision triumphed and the Greek language and culture began to play an increasingly important part in the Middle East. This trend, called Hellenization (after the word 'Hellas' or Greece), had a major impact in Palestine, which was conquered by Alexander the Great in 332 BC.

After the collapse of Alexander's empire, Palestine came under the rule of Hellenistic dynasties. The last of these rulers, Antiochus IV, declared himself a god and looted the temple. Unsurprisingly, in 167 BC, the Jews rebelled. The result was what became called the Maccabean Revolt, from the name of one of its leaders, Judas Maccabeus. The success of this rebellion eventually led to an eighty-year period of Jewish independence.

Despite this independence, the pressures towards Hellenization continued and when, in 63 BC, the expanding Roman Empire took over control of Palestine, these increased. The Romans may have wielded power but their culture around the eastern Mediterranean was very definitely Greek. In fact, the Greek language continued to be the universal language of trade and commerce, especially in the eastern part of the empire. Latin was used only in the army and for official documents.

Impact

Hellenization affected almost every area of life in Palestine. Greek architecture, medicine, philosophy, art and science became important, Greek dress became fashionable and the Greek language became widely spoken. Sometimes

Hellenization was imposed but it also spread of its own accord. If you were upwardly mobile, the Greek way of doing things was very attractive and the key to jobs, education, trade and progress up the social ladder. To a young Jew the choice must have seemed clear: you either stayed in a cultural backwater or you 'went Greek' and experienced the exciting mainstream of the civilized world.

In Jesus' day, the influence of Greek culture was unavoidable, even in Galilee. Four miles to the north of Nazareth lay the Greek-style town of Sepphoris which was being rebuilt in the early part of the first century. We are told that Jesus' stepfather Joseph was a carpenter[1] and as Jesus followed his trade, he may have worked there and been exposed to Greek culture.

Attitudes among the Jews to Hellenization varied. Some aspects of it were recognized as harmless or even welcome; others were much debated. For instance, Greek athletics required nudity and Greek education involved pagan philosophy. To what extent could any real Jew get caught up with either? Some aspects of Hellenization were definitely considered evil by more religious Jews: the Greek temples and theatres portrayed the many Greek gods and goddesses. And the more Hellenized you became, the harder it was to stay ritually pure.*

---

* One side effect of Hellenization was the increasing popularity of the Greek translation of the Old Testament, the Septuagint.

ROMAN POWER

History

When the Romans took over Palestine in 63 BC, they followed what was by now standard operating procedure: they looked for suitable local kings whom they could control and got them to do their dirty work.

After a period of chaos, this policy produced Herod the Great, one of history's more unpleasant characters. Emerging as undisputed king in 37 BC, Herod reigned over a large area until 4 BC. Cunning, greedy, ruthless and wary, Herod suited Roman purposes admirably. Under Herod, the taxes were paid to Rome and troublemakers were speedily and permanently removed. Considered a mere half-Jew by his subjects, Herod preferred Greek culture and delighted in majestic building projects. His most famous achievement – still being built at his death – was the temple in Jerusalem, a structure put up largely to pacify those critics who said that he wasn't a proper Jewish king.

With time, Herod's wariness darkened into a homicidal paranoia. He murdered many people, most notably an uncle, two high priests, a mother-in-law, three sons (including an heir) and his favourite wife. Herod occurs in Matthew's account of the wise men seeking the infant Jesus and the picture of him there – paranoid, deceiving, sensitive about his Jewishness and brutal enough to massacre infants – is true to life.[2]

Herod died in 4 BC* and his kingdom was split into three, portioned out between three surviving sons, Archelaus, Antipas and Philip. At the time of Jesus' ministry, Antipas and Philip were still ruling their portions but Archelaus had been removed by Rome for incompetence. As a result Judea and Samaria were under direct Roman control and were ruled by a series of governors, the most (in)famous being Pontius Pilate.

The Romans were wary of Palestine and the Jews. They never understood the Jews or the Jewish faith and they saw Palestine as an uprising waiting to happen. Inevitably in such a turbulent region, Roman rule was maintained by ruthless methods: a network of informers, the use of immediate arrests and the swift, public and painful execution of agitators.

! ROMAN RULE: A POSTSCRIPT

The crucifixion of Jesus occurred in either AD 30 or 33. What happened in the decades immediately afterwards in Palestine is worth mentioning. These events provide the backdrop to the expansion of the early church and some of Jesus' prophecies of the future centred on them.

---

* The apparent paradox that Herod lived on beyond the birth of Jesus but still managed to die before AD 1 is the result of a miscalculation when the modern calendar was created in the sixth century by the monk Dionysius Exiguus ('Denis the Little').

After the death of the Emperor Tiberius in AD 37, things started to go downhill in Palestine and a succession of incompetent, corrupt and insensitive governors provoked increasing unrest. Finally, in AD 66, a full-scale Jewish rebellion in Palestine flared up. Worried that it might encourage other conquered territories in the empire to rebel, the Romans decided to make an example of the Jews and Jerusalem. In AD 70, Jerusalem was captured and destroyed with enormous loss of life: Josephus, who was an eyewitness, estimated that a million were killed.[3] A hundred thousand Jews were taken captive to Rome and Herod's great temple was levelled. The Jewish War was catastrophic for Judaism and caused changes to faith that have persisted to the present-day. For Christianity, which by AD 70 was a faith spread across the empire, the tragic events of the Jewish revolt had little effect.

Impact

By Jesus' time, a large-scale, full-time army held the sprawling Roman Empire together. This army had to be paid and that meant the conquered states had to pay heavy taxes. Alexander and his compatriots may have had the high vision of spreading Greek culture worldwide, but the Romans just wanted security and taxes. This practical approach meant the Romans were prepared to allow a considerable amount of legal and religious freedom to conquered territories as long as there was no threat to their stability or profitability. It also meant that the Romans were happy to support monsters such as Herod the Great as long as they delivered security and taxes. The implications for the Jewish faith were clear: as long as the money came in and there was no threat of rebellion, the Jews could continue with their religion.

THE JEWISH RESPONSES

The twin threats of Greek culture and Roman power produced a crisis in Judaism. It was impossible to carry out the requirements of the Law in a land run by Romans and full of Greek influence. How could you be a holy nation when you were being corrupted by an alien culture and ruled by an unholy race?

At the time of Jesus, there were several different responses to this crisis. One response was that of *separation*; of trying to be distinctively different from those around you. This was the policy of the *Pharisees*, a group who are prominent in the gospels. The Pharisees appear to have been a pressure group within Judaism focusing on ritual purity and the correct performance of religious practices. They added tradition to the written Law so that no area of life fell outside its rule. The Pharisees' hope seems to have been that if enough people kept God's laws in the proper way, Yahweh would intervene and rescue the nation.

Although Jesus and the Pharisees had much in common, there were conflicts. Jesus criticized the Pharisees because he felt that their vast number of traditions and laws had come to obscure God's Law. The Pharisees objected to Jesus' practice of eating with people whom they considered unclean. They were also uneasy about the way he personally offered people forgiveness. Yet the picture in the gospels is not uniformly negative: for instance, in John's Gospel a Pharisee called Nicodemus is shown to be quite receptive to what Jesus had to say.[4]

A second response to the crisis in Judaism was that of *concession*; of coming to terms with the way things were. This was the policy of the Sadducees, a group that the Pharisees saw as their main opponents. We know little about the Sadducees but they were higher up the social scale than the Pharisees and were based in Jerusalem, where they maintained a profitable control of the temple. The Sadducees only believed in the first five books of the Old Testament and held to none of the Pharisees' additions to the Law. The Sadducees were cautious about the idea that God was going to send a Messiah to save the nation, partly because they didn't believe the later books of the Old Testament and partly because, as aristocrats, they didn't like anything that smacked of a change of power. It was the Sadducees who had the best working arrangement with the Romans.

A third response to the crisis facing the Jews in the Palestine of Jesus' day was that of *rebellion*. Many groups and individuals believed that the only solution to the crisis was to repeat the strategy of the Macabbean Revolt and remove the Romans by force. The best known of such groups were the Zealots, who were heavily involved in guerrilla fighting against Rome in the war of AD 66–73. Although the Zealot party did not formally exist at the time of Jesus, there were many who held to rebellion as the answer. One of Jesus' disciples was 'Simon the Zealot'[5] and Jesus' choice of both him and Matthew the tax collector (and therefore a collaborator with the Romans) as his followers suggests the twelve disciples were a very diverse group. Almost every aspect of Jesus' teaching opposes the idea of rebellion, and the teaching of his followers as recorded in the letters of the New Testament shows no interest whatever in causing political trouble.

A fourth response to the crisis was that of *isolation*. This was the policy of the *Essenes*, a group who, while they existed at the time of Jesus, make no appearance in the pages of the New Testament. The response of the Essenes was to withdraw from society altogether and to create alternative communities where they waited for God to intervene. The famous Dead Sea Scrolls were almost certainly written, or collected, by an Essene group of some kind.

In fact at the time of Jesus, the vast majority of the people, those the gospels refer to as 'the common people' or 'the crowd', probably belonged to none of these groups. Both the Pharisees and the Sadducees were scornful of these 'people of the land'.

The Pharisees' contempt was due to the inability of such ordinary people to keep the Law in the depth and breadth they demanded.[6] The Sadducees' contempt was probably simply snobbery.

It is not hard to guess how the ordinary people lived. They kept the feasts as best they could, tried (and no doubt failed) to keep themselves ritually pure, despaired of the corruption and taxes and looked forward to the long-promised Messiah. They muddled along. If you had to characterize their lives, the best words would probably be *confusion* and *desperation*.

These 'ordinary people' are important for two reasons. Firstly, much of Jesus' teaching was clearly directed at them and they responded enthusiastically to him. Secondly, most of us can identify more easily with these ordinary people, in their confusion and quiet desperation, than with any of the other groups. They are where we are at.

* * *

It is reported that for many years a sign hung in the UN headquarters in southern Lebanon, saying: 'If you understand what's going on here you haven't been properly briefed.' Translated into Latin and shifted nearly two thousand years back in time and a hundred miles south, it could easily have hung in Pontius Pilate's office. Jesus' world was one where turbulent currents of culture, belief and power mingled uneasily.

And yet when you look beyond all the unfamiliar terms and concepts, you see something that was very like our own confused world.

Jesus' Birth

The world that Jesus came to was one in which God's people struggled to survive against hostile forces and, hanging on to his promises, waited for him to intervene. The New Testament tells us that God's intervention, when it occurred, began with the birth of a baby.

PROMISES AND PROPHECIES

The birth of Jesus is described only in the gospels of Matthew and Luke.

Luke's Gospel begins with the birth of John the Baptist. John's parents are an elderly and childless couple: Zechariah, a priest, and his wife Elizabeth. An angel, Gabriel, promises Zechariah that their prayer will be answered and that they will have a son. From Gabriel's promises and the prophecies that Zechariah himself makes, we learn that this boy, John, will grow up to be a great figure, someone who will bring people back to God.[1] Given that there had been no prophets or prophecy for four hundred years, the news that God was going to speak again to Israel must have been astonishing. Even more astonishing is the promise that great though this John will be, his mission will be to point to someone even greater.

Luke then tells how, six months later, the same angel appeared in Nazareth, a village in Galilee, to Mary, a virgin who was engaged to a man called Joseph. Gabriel told Mary she would become pregnant with a son who was to be named Jesus and promised that 'He will be very great and will be called the Son of the Most High. And the Lord God will give him the throne of his ancestor David. And he will reign over Israel for ever; his Kingdom will never end!'[2] In answer to Mary's query as to how this was to happen, given that she was a virgin, Gabriel said to her: 'The Holy Spirit will come upon you, and the power of the Most High will overshadow you. So the baby born to you will be holy, and he will be called the Son of God.'[3]

Matthew tells us that an angel appeared to Joseph and told him that the Holy Spirit had conceived the child that Mary was bearing. He will be called Jesus, 'for he will save his people from their sins.'[4] Jesus, or Yeshua ('Joshua'), was a popular name of the time: besides meaning 'The LORD (Yahweh) saves', it also commemorated the great military hero of the Old Testament who gained the Promised Land for God's people. A further comment by Matthew is also significant: Jesus is to be 'Immanuel', which means 'God with us'.

These early chapters of Luke and Matthew are crammed full of references to the Old Testament. This reminds us that in Jesus the story of the Old Testament continues and finds its fulfilment. You sometimes hear the New Testament represented as if it was something that cancelled the Old Testament, as though God had scrapped Plan A and decided to start again with Plan B. The reality is otherwise: the New Testament sees Jesus not as cancelling the Old Testament but as fulfilling it. These Old Testament links also imply that to understand fully who Jesus was, we have to know something of what happened before.

THE VIRGINAL CONCEPTION

The belief that Jesus was born of a virgin is one of those issues that have become a test case for belief. One problem is that the common term 'the virgin birth of Jesus' is misleading. It is Jesus' conception, not his birth, which is the issue. Both Matthew and Luke[5] are clear that neither Joseph nor any other man was responsible for Jesus' conception: it was God. The 'virginal conception' of Jesus is a better term. The idea that Jesus was born of a virgin is often ridiculed. Some people allege that the whole thing rests on a rather primitive naivety. They suggest that as these first-century authors did not have our knowledge of fertilization, their accounts can be dismissed. This, of course, is nonsense: Joseph may not have known much about gynaecology but he knew that the production of a baby needed a man!

Other people question the account on different grounds. Some point out that many of the Greek or Roman gods were in the habit of having sexual relations with women. True, but three points need making. The first is to question whether anybody ever really took the idea of the gods engaging in sexual activities seriously. The second is that the gospel accounts are very Jewish documents; while tales of the gods engaging in sex occurred amongst the Greeks and Romans, the idea of Yahweh doing anything similar would have been an appalling blasphemy to Jews. Thirdly, the biblical accounts are very different from the lurid Greek or Roman 'gods have sex with woman!' tales. What happens is depicted here as fact, rather than myth, and is described in a way that deliberately avoids any hint of immorality. Mary is promised that 'the Holy Spirit will come upon you, and the power of the Most High will overshadow you'[6] and we are told no more. We get a picture of God being involved in Jesus' conception in a way that is mysterious, awesome, pure and – above all – holy.

Still others argue that the key is to be found in Matthew, where we read: 'All of this happened to fulfil the Lord's message through his prophet: "Look! The virgin will conceive a child! She will give birth to a son, and he will be called Immanuel" (meaning, God is with us).'[7]

What has happened, the sceptics say, is that the idea of Jesus being 'born of a virgin' came about as an attempt to make events fit a prophecy in Isaiah.[8] Yet the idea that Jesus was born of a virgin is also found in Luke and is hinted at elsewhere. A careful reading of the gospels suggests that it was widely known that there was something unusual about Jesus' origins. So, in John we read of a crowd making an insinuation that Jesus is illegitimate[9] and in Mark 6:3 there is no mention of Joseph as Jesus' father. Furthermore, Jesus was known as 'Jesus, Son of Mary', which is very striking in a culture where a child is always known as the son or daughter of their father.

Of course, some sceptics have suggested that this hint of illegitimacy was there for the most obvious reasons: Jesus *was* illegitimate. In our culture, where nearly fifty per cent of all births are now outside marriage, such an allegation is easy to believe. But while illegitimacy may have occurred in rural Palestine in Jesus' day, it would have been very unlikely in the sort of small religious village where everybody knows everybody else and a woman can barely glance at a man without it being noticed. And Jewish culture and law valued virginity highly.

Behind these real objections to a virginal conception seems to be the old contention: miracles cannot happen. But once you accept there is a God who can, and does, intervene in his world, then the difficulties vanish. If Jesus was in some way divine, then God has to get involved in the human story at some point and conception is the obvious place.

But why did God have to do it this way? Why did he become a human in Jesus? The Christian view is that the human race needs rescuing from the mess it is in, but that any rescuer must have both the power and the right to intervene. Someone who was merely human couldn't act as rescuer: they would, by definition, be part of the problem. And someone who was 'merely' God would not be entitled to save us; he would not be one of us. Jesus represents the answer to this problem: as 'God become one of us', he is *eligible* to save us and yet also has the *power* to save us. The virginal conception allows Jesus to have the necessary dual citizenship of both heaven and earth.

There is another point. It is easy to be intimidated by the idea of God. Yet one aspect of the Christmas story is that God came to earth in this way so that he wouldn't intimidate us. God didn't become bigger to impress us, he became smaller to attract us.

THE CHRISTMAS STORY

When was Jesus born? It was no earlier than 6 BC, because Luke says that Jesus was 'about thirty' when he began his ministry around AD 27 or 28, and no later than 4 BC, because that's when Herod the Great died.* Incidentally, we have no real way of knowing the date of Jesus' birth. It was Constantine, the first Christian Roman emperor, who ruled in AD 336 that 25 December should be celebrated as Christ's birthday, a date chosen to replace a pagan mid-winter festival.

Both Matthew and Luke state that Jesus was born in Bethlehem, a small town about eight kilometres (five miles) to the south-west of Jerusalem. Although Mary and Joseph lived in Nazareth, their presence in Bethlehem is explained as being due to a census ordered by Caesar Augustus** that required registration at an ancestral town. In Joseph's case this was Bethlehem, the city of King David. Luke tells us that Jesus' birthplace was humble; he was cradled among the animals.

---

* The 'star' that, in Matthew's Gospel, led the wise men to Jesus has proved to be a tantalising, but so far unhelpful, clue. If we could identify it as a comet, a supernova or some arrangement of astrologically significant stars, we might be able to use it to get a better date but (despite endless theories) its identity is still elusive.

** The census is one of a handful of claimed historical discrepancies in the gospels, as the only known census of Quirinius was much later, around AD 6–9. So did Luke get his facts wrong? It seems improbable: Luke is very accurate on Roman history and such a careless blunder is unlike him. There are several possible explanations but we simply don't know enough to be sure which, if any, is correct.

The long-sought king comes but is born in poverty: the hinge of history is to be found on the door of a Bethlehem stable.

In this most basic of settings, Mary and Joseph were visited by shepherds who had been summoned there by angels. Shepherds were close to the bottom of the social ladder and the fact that it is they, not the social and religious elite of Jerusalem, who were called by the angels is significant. Jesus was to be good news for the poor and those on the margins of society.

Although the 'three kings' often appear in nativity plays, the Bible simply tells us[10] that these other visitors were 'Magi' or 'wise men' rather than kings, and says nothing about how many there were or whether they represented different races. It does not even tell us that they visited the baby in the manger; it tells us instead that they visited a child in a house. So their visit may have been much later. These 'Magi', who probably came from the area of modern Iraq or Iran, studied the stars in the hope that they revealed the future. The idea that such people should travel for months to find a Jewish Messiah may seem unlikely. Yet intriguingly, two separate Roman authors, Suetonius and Tacitus, mention that there was a widespread belief that a world ruler would come from the Jewish people.* So a Jewish king could have been seen as of more than local significance.

---

* Suetonius, *The Lives of the Caesars, Vespasian* 4; Tacitus, *The Histories* 5:13.

The attitude of the Magi is in stark contrast with those of Herod and the priests. The Magi knew very little about the Messiah but chose to travel vast distances to show him honour. Herod and the priests had all the knowledge and resources of the Jewish faith available, yet failed to see what was happening just a few miles away. When they did find out, they reacted with apathy and hostility.

The fact that the priests failed to seek out Jesus for themselves and that Herod sought him to kill him reminds us that not all Jews were looking forward to the Messiah's coming. The priests' apathy can be attributed to three factors. First, under the rule of the increasingly paranoid Herod, any speculation about the Messiah was very definitely off the agenda. Second, the temple leadership was dominated by the worldly and upper-class Sadducees who were more concerned with practical matters than with any idea of a Messiah. Some of the senior priests were probably Roman appointees and chosen precisely because they had no interest in anything (such as a Messiah) that would get in the way of Roman rule. And third, staying alive under Herod and managing the profitable temple franchise must have kept them busy. It would not be the first – or last – time that running a religious enterprise got in the way of discovering God's purposes.

Matthew tells us that shortly after the visit of the Magi, King Herod, anxious to remove any threat to his dynasty, ordered the massacre of all infants of two and under in

Bethlehem. Although unrecorded elsewhere, the massacre at Bethlehem is consistent with the obsessive and psychopathic paranoia of Herod's terrible last years. Mary and Joseph fled to Egypt with Jesus, before returning to Nazareth in Galilee after Herod's death.

! ISSUES WITH ANGELS

As we have seen, angels occur several times in the account of Jesus' birth. Today the idea of angels attracts two extreme points of view. On the one hand, those sceptical of the miraculous treat any mention of angels as a myth. On the other hand, much of modern Western society is now rapidly acquiring mystical beliefs that have an uncritical fascination with angels. A careful reading of all the Bible says (and does not say) on the subject of angels is an essential counterbalance to both the incredulity of scepticism and the credulity of mysticism.

Angels appear at major events in Jesus' life; Jesus believed in the existence of angels and he talked about them frequently.[11] The main role of angels seems to be to serve God as his faithful agents, acting as his servants, messengers and sometimes warriors. The Bible tells us that angels are powerful living creatures created by God, spiritual beings who, while they do not have physical bodies, can take on human appearance. There is something awesome and almost terrifying about angels.

Normally when the Bible talks about angels, it refers to those who are good and holy. Some angels, however, have rebelled against God and are evil. The leader of these fallen angels is the devil, or Satan.

The role of angels as protectors and helpers of God's people continues. There are many reports, often from solid, reliable witnesses, of mysterious helpers or defenders appearing to God's people at times of crisis or need and then suddenly vanishing. Angels may have a bigger role in life than we imagine.

In John's Gospel there is no description of Jesus' birth but instead an extraordinary prologue in which John reflects on the meaning of Jesus' coming.[12] In a deliberate echo of the very first words of the Old Testament, he says that the whole creation was made by 'the Word', someone who 'was with God and was God'. This 'Word', says John, is not just the maker of all things, he is also 'light and life', the source of everything that is essential for existence. Then, in one of the most awesome statements ever written by anybody, anywhere, John says this: 'So the Word became human and lived here on earth among us.'[13] In Jesus, God – the eternal Word – became flesh and blood.

Yet John also points out something that is both surprising and disturbing. He says this about Jesus: 'Although the world was made through him, the world didn't recognize him when he came. Even in his own land and among his own people, he was not accepted. But to all who believed him and accepted him, he gave the right to become children of God.'[14]

Here is the real issue of the story of Jesus' birth. Jesus' coming was not an automatic blessing on all humanity. It is all too easy to ignore or reject Jesus. Yet to recognize Jesus for who he is; to accept him as the Word made a human being is, as John says, to be given the wonderful right and privilege of being a child of God and knowing God as your heavenly father.

THE BEGINNINGS OF JESUS' MINISTRY

The gospels reveal little about what happened in Jesus' life until he began his ministry of teaching and healing. According to the dating given by Luke,[1] John the Baptist began to preach in AD 27, with Jesus' own ministry starting soon afterwards. This means that around thirty years had elapsed since the events in Bethlehem. What happened during that time?

THE LONG SILENCE

The only incident recorded during this time in Jesus' life is one mentioned by Luke: a memorable visit to Jerusalem with his parents when Jesus was twelve. He concludes that account with this: 'Then Jesus returned to Nazareth with them and was obedient to them; and his mother stored all these things in her heart. So Jesus grew both in height and in wisdom, and he was loved by God and by all who knew him.'[2]

The implication is that Jesus grew up normally in a life largely indistinguishable from that of any other child in the village. Like most Jewish boys raised in devout Jewish families, Jesus would have been taught to read the Old Testament and would have memorized large portions of it. He would probably also have followed common practice and learned Joseph's trade of carpenter or builder (the Greek word can mean either).[3]

It seems that people have always found the limited nature of this information rather unsatisfactory and there are many legendary accounts that seek to plug the gap. The attraction of such documents persists. Every so often a book gets written with a title such as 'Jesus: the Hidden Years' and – as a subtitle – one of those eye-catching questions such as 'Did Jesus travel to India and learn the Ancient Wisdom of the Gurus?' to which the true answer is inevitably 'No'. The fact is that although what Jesus taught was remarkable and unparalleled within Judaism, it shows no signs of being influenced by anything outside the Jewish faith.

The reality is, no doubt, that Jesus grew up, was educated in his faith and followed Joseph's trade, and that very little else happened. The idea that for a large part of his earthly existence Jesus lived a life in which little happened ought to be an encouragement to the many people who find themselves in situations that do not change as fast as they would like. God is the master of events and also non-events.

There is, however, one observation worth making. When, after this long gap, the gospel writers talk of Jesus' family, Joseph is no longer present and it is assumed that he had died in the meantime. So Jesus probably knew something of family bereavement. But it is significant that with Joseph's death, Jesus – as the eldest son – would have become head of a family which by now included Mary and at least six other children.[4] Many people, faced with the burden of family responsibilities, can be inclined to say to God: 'You know nothing of all this'. Yet, despite being unmarried and not having children, Jesus probably did know something of bearing the responsibility for a family. Here too, he can sympathize.[5]

JOHN THE BAPTIST AND THE ANNOUNCEMENT OF THE KING AND THE KINGDOM

All the gospels link the beginning of Jesus' ministry with John the Baptist, a figure they view as very important. History agrees. Josephus mentions John as a baptizer and a moral reformer and says that he had such an extraordinary impact on the Jewish people that Herod Antipas became worried that he might incite a revolt.[6] Jesus gave John the highest praise, saying that he was 'more than a prophet' and that he was 'the greatest man who had ever lived'.[7]

So who was John the Baptist? Firstly, John was a prophet[8] and was recognized as one by the public.[9] His rough dress of camel's hair, his diet of locusts and wild honey, his base in the desert and, not least, his thundering denunciations of Jewish society led many to see him as a prophet in the mould of Elijah, the most dramatic of the Old Testament prophets. Some people even believed that John actually was Elijah.

The fact that John's claim to be a prophet was accepted is significant; it must have sent a wave of excitement through the nation. After centuries of silence, prophecy had returned: God was speaking to Israel again. One of the chief tasks of a prophet was to condemn evil and injustice and get Israel back on course as the covenant-keeping people of God. John did this and was a prophet of national repentance. His preaching focused on the futility of relying on God's covenant when you didn't keep it. Being one of God's people was a privilege with a responsibility, and a right relationship with God meant there had to be right actions: belief and behaviour went together. So John told the crowd to share clothing and food, tax collectors not to demand more than was their right and soldiers not to bully people.[10]

No one was spared from John's denunciations. He criticized religious leaders and even denounced Herod Antipas, the 'king' of Galilee, for marrying his brother's wife. It was a challenge that predictably led to John's imprisonment.

Yet John didn't just preach the need for urgent repentance before God's judgement fell: he announced that the long-promised Messiah, God's king, was near. Later, when Jesus came to John, he said that Jesus was the one he had spoken of.[11] John also added something that must have seemed mysterious to his hearers: Jesus was 'the Lamb of God who takes away the sin of the world'.[12]

John also promised the coming of the Kingdom of God.*[13] The Kingdom of God is God's reign and rule over people and nations, the rule that sets people free from the control of evil and brings them into the blessings of God's power and presence. The idea that God's king would bring about God's kingdom was widespread: the two ideas went together and Jesus himself was to say a lot more about both.

The most distinctive feature of what John did and said is the baptizing that gave him his title. He baptized – or ritually washed – those who came to him in the Jordan River. Washing was a part of Jewish life; it was essential to keeping the laws of ritual purity. Yet John's baptism appears to have been different. It was the sort of washing that a non-Jew would have done as part of conversion to Judaism but John required baptism *of Jews*. It was a startling way of saying that it was not enough to be descended from Abraham. To be a real Jew, to be part of God's people, there had to be conversion, a deliberate turning

---

* Matthew talks about the 'Kingdom of Heaven' in his gospel but it means the same thing; strict Jews often used the word 'Heaven' to avoid using the word 'God', which they considered too holy to be spoken.

to God marked by an act of baptism and a new life character-ized by right actions.

John's baptism also looked forward to the Messiah: it was an act that signified not just repentance but also expectancy. Through it, John created a body of people who were eagerly waiting for God's king to appear. Some of John's disciples even-tually became those of Jesus and no doubt many of those who were baptized by John sought out Jesus and listened to him.

JESUS' BAPTISM

The synoptic gospels record that Jesus was baptized by John the Baptist in the Jordan River.[14] Mark's account is a good summary of what happened: 'One day Jesus came from Nazareth in Galilee, and he was baptized by John in the River Jordan. And when Jesus came up out of the water, he saw the heavens split open and the Holy Spirit descending like a dove on him. And a voice came from heaven saying, "You are my beloved Son, and I am fully pleased with you."'[15]

The key to the significance of Jesus' baptism is the voice from heaven that confirms his identity as God's Son and declares that God is pleased with him. That is something that obvi-ously must have been important to Jesus. 'You are my beloved Son, and I am fully pleased with you' is a combination of two separate Old Testament verses, each of which is significant. The first is from a psalm to do with the coronation of God's king:

'The king proclaims the LORD's decree: "The LORD said to me, 'you are my son. Today I have become your Father."'[16]

The second is from a passage in the Old Testament prophecy of Isaiah about the mysterious Servant figure who is to come and who, by suffering, will save God's people and bring global justice: 'Look at my servant, whom I strengthen. He is my chosen one, and I am pleased with him. I have put my Spirit upon him. He will reveal justice to the nations.'[17]

Taken together, these verses not only confirm that Jesus is the Messiah but also suggest the sort of Messiah he is going to be. Jesus is going to be both the king of God's people *and* the Servant who, through his suffering, brings justice to the world.

Yet there are other things: the heavens being 'torn open' and the Spirit descending 'like a dove' are images that suggest that God has poured out his presence, blessing and power on Jesus through the Holy Spirit. The Holy Spirit is the divine agent who carries out God's purposes in the world and who strengthens God's people. That Jesus was filled with the Spirit at his baptism fulfilled a great prophecy of the Messiah in Isaiah that 'the Spirit of the LORD will rest on him'.[18] Practically, it is significant that even God's Son did not begin his work without being empowered and anointed* by the Holy Spirit. Jesus, in

---

* The idea of 'anointing' is significant. The word *Messiah* meant 'Anointed One', a reference to the oil that was symbolically poured on the head of a new king (see 1Kings 1:39).

turn, insisted that his disciples follow this pattern, instructing them to wait in Jerusalem until they were baptized with the Holy Spirit.[19] Many of the unhappy events and failed ventures that have marred the history of the Christian church over the years can be attributed to a recurrent habit of people trying to do things without the Spirit's power.

The baptism of Jesus is an event where God the Father confirms Jesus' authority and identity as his Son and empowers him for his ministry as the Messiah through the Spirit. At his baptism, Jesus' vocation was confirmed.

THE TESTING OF JESUS

The gospels tell us that Jesus' baptism by John was followed by his temptation by the devil. If Jesus' baptism marked the start of his ministry, the temptation marked his first testing.

The synoptic gospels tell how, immediately after his baptism, Jesus spent forty days in the wilderness – the desert – where he was tempted. The period of forty days is a reminder of the history of the Jewish people: Moses had also spent forty days and nights fasting in the wilderness before receiving God's Law[20] and the Israelites had spent forty years in the wilderness after being disobedient to God. Jesus' time in the desert will mark him out not only as the new Moses, but also as the representative of the new Israel, the people who are obedient in the wilderness.

It is not hard to see the issues facing Jesus at this time. Through his baptism, Jesus has just been commissioned and anointed as the Messiah: now, in the wilderness, he has to decide *how* he is going to be the Messiah. To understand what Jesus faced in the wilderness, we need to understand the relationship between 'being tested' and 'being tempted'. Both terms are used of this experience of Jesus. To *test* something or someone is to do something positive: the tester hopes the test will be passed so there can be a progression to some new stage. But to *tempt* someone is a much more negative action: the tempter hopes the temptation will be failed. Now, if you take the Bible's view that there is both a God and a devil in the universe, then you can see how something can be both a test and a temptation. From God's perspective, this time in the wilderness was a *test* for Jesus, because he wanted his Son to succeed. From the devil's standpoint it was an opportunity to *tempt* Jesus, because he wanted him to fail.

Linked with this is the way that all the accounts of Jesus' temptation talk of him being 'led' or 'compelled' by the Holy Spirit to go into the wilderness and face the devil. Jesus was not, as it were, quietly minding his own business when he was set upon by the devil. His testing was the result of God's initiative in sending Jesus to battle with the devil on his home territory, the wilderness. There are two important points here that are relevant, not just to the life of Jesus but to all history. Firstly, God, not the devil, is in charge of events. Secondly, Jesus was not just someone who managed to endure the attacks of the devil but someone who challenged him, fought him and won. Jesus is not merely the great survivor of evil: he is the ultimate victor over it.

! DEALING WITH THE DEVIL

No one who reads the accounts of Jesus' temptation can overlook the fact that they are all about his encounter with a living, personal, supernatural opponent, the devil. Here, as elsewhere in the gospels, there is a mention of an evil, spiritual adversary.

In thinking about Satan, or the devil,* we need to put out of our minds any ideas of red suits, forked tails and horns. There is none of that in the Bible. What we learn there is that the devil is the chief of those angelic powers who are opposed to God and his people.

The devil is mentioned rarely in the Bible. However, the fact that most of the references to the devil are found in the teaching of Jesus should caution us against dismissing any idea of him as a mere superstition. The devil is both the great enemy of the Kingdom of God and the one who tempts human beings. From the references to the devil in the gospels, we can learn the following things:

---

* *Satan* comes from a Hebrew word meaning 'the adversary' and *the devil* is from the Greek equivalent, *diabolos*. The two words are used interchangeably in the gospels. The devil has other titles in the gospels including 'the Tempter', 'Beelzebub' and 'the Enemy'.

First, the devil is powerful. Jesus called him the 'prince of this world',[21] implying that the world is under his influence.

Second, the devil is always hostile towards us. He is 'the evil one' that we are to pray to be delivered from and the one who snatches away the good news from people's hearts.[22] Jesus also described the devil as being a 'murderer'.[23]

Third, the devil's methods are deceitful. Jesus said of the devil that he 'hates the truth' and 'is a liar', and that he 'is the father of lies'.[24] Elsewhere, Jesus portrays Satan as being like an evil farmer who secretly sows weeds in the fields of a rival.[25]

Yet for all their portrayal of the devil as being powerful, hostile and deceitful, the gospels also show him as someone whose power and menace are limited. He is never seen as an excuse for human evil (as in 'the devil made me do it') but as someone who, with God's power, we can resist. Jesus' actions of exorcism and healing demonstrated his superiority over the devil. Yet Jesus' challenge to the devil was far more than a few specific demonstrations of power a long time ago in Palestine. Jesus taught that the cross was where the devil's power would be decisively destroyed: 'The time of judgement for the world has come, when the prince of this world will be cast out.'[26]

The letters of the New Testament expand on the teaching of Jesus[27] and, in particular, make much of the fact the devil is now a defeated foe.[28]

The testing of Jesus involved three separate temptations:

The temptation to turn stones into bread

'If you are the Son of God, change these stones into loaves of bread.'[29]

The first temptation addresses Jesus' physical appetite. On one level, it is an attack at a point where Jesus is weakest: he has been fasting for a long time. Yet the temptation is more subtle than it seems. The devil was trying to raise doubts in Jesus' mind about whether he was the Son of God and whether he really did have miraculous powers. At an even deeper level, there is another challenge: whether Jesus should use his powers independently of his Father's will for his own benefit. Jesus' response was to quote the Old Testament: 'People need more than bread for their life; real life comes by feeding on every word of the LORD.'[30] Jesus quoted the Bible here not because it has any magic power (the devil quotes it too) but because in this verse, God promises that trusting in him is the most important thing in life.

The temptation to leap from the highest point of the temple

'Then the Devil took him to Jerusalem, to the highest point of the Temple, and said, "If you are the Son of God, jump off! For the Scriptures say, 'He orders his angels to protect you. And they will hold you with their hands to keep you from striking your foot on a stone.'"'[31]

The devil now takes Jesus to the heights of the temple and, quoting Scripture, suggests that he throw himself down. While this may be a temptation for Jesus to prove that he is the Messiah by some stunning public demonstration, it is far more likely that it is another attempt to make Jesus doubt his status as God's son. 'Prove it,' the devil is saying. 'If God really is your caring Father, he will protect you.'

Jesus' reply is again brief, blunt and based on the Bible: 'The Scriptures also say, "Do not test the Lord your God."'[32] The quote, again from Deuteronomy,[33] refers to the Israelites being unfaithful and rebellious against God in the wilderness. By referring to it, Jesus is announcing his refusal to do what they did. He trusts in his Father's loving care and has no need to test it.

The temptation to worship the devil

'Next the Devil took him to the peak of a very high mountain and showed him the nations of the world and all their glory. "I will give it all to you," he said, "if you will only kneel down and worship me."'[34]

The devil finally took Jesus to where he could see all the kingdoms of the world and offered them to him. It is the most blatant of all the temptations, as if, having run out of options, the devil puts all his cards on the table. The offer is attractive: it is for Jesus to seize his inheritance without obedience to God's plan. Behind it is the temptation to take the short cut, to try to gain glory without sacrifice. Jesus' reply is a final rejection: "'Get out of here, Satan,' Jesus told him. "For the Scriptures say, 'You must worship the Lord your God; serve only him.'"" [35] The passage Jesus quotes (Deuteronomy 6:13) refers to exactly the sort of idolatry that he is now rejecting. Jesus has determined that whatever it costs, his ministry will be carried out in God's way.

Luke tells us that 'When the Devil had finished tempting Jesus, he left him until the next opportunity came.' [36] Jesus had won a victory which determined the shape of his ministry, but the devil had not been permanently defeated. Jesus would face temptation again.

JESUS'
MINISTRY

Three phases can be identified in Jesus' ministry. In the first phase, Jesus was based in Judea (the southern part of Palestine), visited Jerusalem several times and had only a few disciples on an informal basis. In the second phase, Jesus was based in Galilee, where he called the twelve disciples, preached publicly on a large scale and performed numerous miracles. In the third phase of his ministry, Jesus left Galilee and moved south to Judea and the adjacent area of Perea for a final period of teaching before going to Jerusalem to face arrest, trial and execution.

When did this happen? From what Luke[1] tells us, it seems that Jesus started his ministry around AD 27–29. The exact year of the crucifixion is debated, with the two probable dates being AD 30 or 33. The most likely scenario seems to be that Jesus began his ministry in the latter part of AD 27 and was crucified on the Friday of the Passover of AD 30, which fell that year on 7 April. That we can be so certain about the precise date of Jesus' death is a reminder that we are dealing with a real person and historic events; we are a long way from the world of myth.

THE FIRST PHASE: THE EARLY MINISTRY

Covered in John 1:15–5:47.
Probable dates: late AD 27 into AD 28.

From the first five chapters of John we learn that Jesus spent time in Judea and Jerusalem before his main ministry in Galilee. During this period, Jesus performed miracles, taught about eternal life, made references to his own death and resurrection and had some dealings with Jewish leaders, Samaritans and Gentiles. In Jerusalem, among those who should have received him gladly, Jesus found rejection and opposition. Despite John the Baptist's preaching and his own teaching and miracles in Jerusalem, the nation had not repented. The failure of Israel to repent seems to have been critical in determining what happened next. When John the Baptist was imprisoned, Jesus returned to Galilee and there he began a new course of action: he called twelve disciples to follow him.

THE SECOND PHASE: THE MINISTRY IN THE NORTH

Covered in Matthew 4:12–18:35; Mark 1:14–9:50; Luke 4:14 –9:50; probably John 6:1–10:21.

Probable dates: late AD 28–autumn AD 29.

This second phase marks the beginning of the main part of Jesus' ministry. Having been rejected by the religious leadership in Jerusalem, he began to gather a new people of God. The nucleus of that new community was the twelve disciples. In this new phase, Jesus was based in Galilee and only towards the end of this time did he move beyond it.

Jesus chose for his base Capernaum, a fishing village on the shores of the Sea of Galilee, and he drew at least four of his closest followers from Capernaum's commercial fishermen. Having access to a boat (and the men able to sail it) provided Jesus with an invaluable escape route when the crowds got too large. A short sail eastwards from Capernaum allowed him to leave the territory of Herod Antipas and 'cross the state line' into the territory of Herod Philip or that of the independent confederation of the Decapolis ('the Ten Towns') on the other side of the lake.

After John the Baptist's imprisonment, Jesus went to Capernaum and began to call people to follow him. Jesus had known such people as Simon Peter, Andrew, Philip and Nathaniel before,[2] but he now issued a call for them to follow him permanently. Soon Jesus had gathered twelve men as his disciples and had many other followers. Jesus began his public teaching in the synagogues and began teaching around Galilee in a ministry that combined preaching and healing. Soon he was preaching to crowds numbering thousands.[3]

Mark tells us what Jesus said: '"At last the time has come!" he announced. "The Kingdom of God is near! Turn from your sins and believe this Good News!"'[4] Soon Jesus' teaching began to focus on explaining what the Kingdom was and the demands that it made on people.

The gospels are clear that Jesus did not just teach; he also performed miracles. These were primarily miracles of healing but they also included 'nature miracles': demonstrations of power and authority over such things as wind and waves, bread and wine. These were actions – 'signs' – that highlighted and authenticated Jesus' teaching.

At first, Jesus' ministry appears to have had almost universal support yet, increasingly, opposition mounted. It is easy to recognize a pattern of reactions among the religious authorities in Galilee: at first they are puzzled by Jesus, and then, in rapid succession, they become uneasy, irritated and – finally – hostile.

At some point during Jesus' ministry in Galilee, Herod Antipas had John the Baptist executed. This event, and the rise in religious antagonism, triggered a change in Jesus' ministry. From then on, Jesus adopted a more itinerant style, moving around Galilee or crossing the Sea of Galilee by boat. Increasingly, we see Jesus using parables as a way of teaching.

Jesus faced two threats at this time. His most obvious peril came from his enemies. More and more, as Jesus taught, healed or just ate meals with people, he found himself watched with disapproval by people who asked him critical questions. A second and more subtle threat came from his friends. Particularly amongst the crowds, there was such enthusiasm for Jesus that there was a risk of things getting out of hand. A real danger existed that the crowd would publicly declare Jesus the Messiah on their terms and would start a popular uprising with catastrophic consequences. On one occasion at least, things evidently came close to this. When Jesus miraculously fed a vast number of people (five thousand men and an uncounted number of women and children),[5] the crowd's response was to want to make him king by force.[6] Jesus' reaction was immediate: he dismissed the crowd, sent the disciples back across the Sea of Galilee and then left to go into the hills to pray alone.[7]

The existence of these two threats helps explain what Jesus said and did. He was careful to avoid saying anything that explicitly declared he was the Messiah: that word had acquired so many political and revolutionary overtones that its careless use had to be avoided. No doubt for the same reason, Jesus played down some of his miracles, even telling those who were healed not to talk about what had happened.[8] And when hostility loomed or popular enthusiasm seemed about to bubble over, Jesus' response was to move on and let things settle down.

After what seems to have been a particularly serious dispute over his relaxed attitude to ritual purity,[9] Jesus took the disciples north to the Gentile regions of Tyre and Sidon. In doing this, Jesus was not just avoiding further controversy; he was also deliberately preparing the way for the mission to the Gentiles that the disciples would undertake after the resurrection.

THE TURNING POINT

Jesus' activities in Galilee ended after three very significant and linked events that occurred within a week.

The first event took place near 'the villages of Caesarea Philippi',[10] just beyond the northernmost limit of Galilee. There Jesus asked the disciples who people thought he was and received from Simon Peter the answer, 'You are the Messiah, the Son of the living God.'[11] It was clearly a significant moment: after months of following Jesus, the leader of the Twelve had stated his belief that Jesus was the great long-promised deliverer of God's people.

The second event followed immediately afterwards, as Jesus told them for the first time that he would 'suffer many terrible things and be rejected by the leaders, the leading priests, and the teachers of religious law. He would be killed, and three days later he would rise again.'[12] His announcement that as Messiah he would suffer humiliation and shame rather than triumph and honour was instantly rejected.[13] All the popular conceptions of a Messiah featured a glorious and powerful king: the idea of a Messiah who would suffer was both unfamiliar and disagreeable. Even as the Twelve were digesting this almost incomprehensible statement, Jesus followed it with something even worse. If they wanted to follow him, he said, they must put aside their own selfish ambition, shoulder their cross and be prepared to die.[14] Not only was Jesus going to suffer as Messiah, but those who wanted to follow him should be prepared to take the same hard road.

Over the next few days, two questions must have gone through the disciples' minds. First, in view of what Jesus had said about his future, could he really be the Messiah? Second, given what Jesus had said about the cost of being a disciple, did they want to follow him even if he was the Messiah?

This atmosphere of confusion, doubt and fear provides the background for the third event, which occurred a week later. This event is the transfiguration, one of the most dramatic and mysterious events in the New Testament. According to the gospels,[15] Jesus took three disciples, Peter, James and John, up a mountain to pray. There Jesus' appearance changed 'so that his face shone like the sun, and his clothing became dazzling white'.[16] Suddenly Moses and Elijah, the two great figures of the Old Testament, appeared and began talking with Jesus 'of how he was about to fulfil God's plan by dying in Jerusalem'.[17] Peter, who had a habit of speaking first and thinking later, suggested that they set up three shelters. But even as he spoke, a bright cloud appeared with God's voice declaring from it, 'This is my beloved Son, and I am fully pleased with him. Listen to him.'[18] The two figures departed, leaving only Jesus.

What is the significance of the transfiguration? At the time, the most important thing was that it confirmed to the perplexed disciples that, for all their concerns, Jesus was indeed the Messiah and should be listened to. Yet what they saw also demonstrated what Peter had declared: Jesus was the Son of God, someone who was more than a human being. It was a lesson the disciples needed to learn.

The whole account of the transfiguration is full of echoes of the Old Testament. Moses and Elijah stand for the two great divisions of the Old Testament, the Law and the Prophets; the encounter was similar to Moses' meeting with God on Mount Sinai[19] and the cloud was like that which was often associated with God's presence.[20] These echoes are vital. They show that the suffering that Jesus said he would undergo in Jerusalem was not a distortion of the divine plan for the Messiah: it was the true plan.

There is one other significant aspect to the transfiguration. It was not a changing of Jesus from what he was into what he wasn't; it was the opposite: a revelation of Jesus as he really is. Inevitably, the gospels focus on Jesus as the human being, the one who lived in obscurity and who died in shameful and painful weakness on the cross. Yet in the transfiguration, for a moment, the disguise was dropped and the disciples saw something of Jesus, the awesome Son of God, full of glory, majesty and honour.[21]

After the transfiguration, Jesus returned with his disciples to Galilee for a brief period. Things were now different, however; there was a change in emphasis in Jesus' activities. In order to teach the disciples he now sought privacy.[22] Back in Galilee, Jesus gave a second prophecy of his death and resurrection, only this time there was a new and alarming addition: 'he would be betrayed.'[23] Then, possibly in the late autumn of AD 29, Jesus and the disciples left Galilee. Knowing what the consequences would be, Jesus led his followers south towards Judea and Jerusalem.

THE THIRD PHASE: THE MINISTRY IN THE SOUTH

Covered in Matthew 19:1–20:34; Mark 10:1–52; Luke 9:51–19:27; John 10:22–12:11.
Probable dates: late autumn AD 29–end March AD 30.

There are two fixed points in this phase. The first is that, as John tells us,[24] Jesus made an appearance in Jerusalem for the Festival of Dedication (Hanukkah) in December and, after nearly being arrested, he returned to the other side of the Jordan. The second is that, whether we pick AD 30 or AD 33 as the year of the crucifixion, Passover fell in each case in early

April, and Jesus was on the outskirts of Jerusalem shortly before the beginning of the feast.

Taking all the evidence, it seems that shortly after the turning point of Peter's declaration and the transfiguration, Jesus and the Twelve left Galilee and made their way south. They crossed the River Jordan and spent some time in Perea, the Jewish territory east of the Jordan.[25] Matthew and Luke tell us that Jesus travelled south not just with the Twelve but with other followers, including women.[26] The mood of the party was darkened by Jesus making a third prophecy of his death and resurrection.[27] This was the most explicit prediction yet; Jesus referred to himself being handed over to the Gentiles, mocked, flogged and crucified. The accounts make it clear that Jesus knew what he faced in Jerusalem; they are equally clear that the disciples did not understand what he was talking about.

From Perea, Jesus and his followers made periodic excursions to Jerusalem. Jesus had friends at Bethany, half an hour's walk from Jerusalem, who hosted both him and the disciples on several occasions during these last months.[28] The impression we get of Jesus' activities at this time is that although he was still healing people and teaching in public, his priority was to spend time with his disciples. When Jesus did meet the religious authorities, the encounters were always hostile and the questions posed to him were only rarely genuine enquiries; they were more commonly trick questions designed to trap him.

This hostility raises an important question: why did Jesus meet opposition? The answer is that people opposed Jesus for many reasons:

- While Jesus was unshakeable in his dedication to God's Law as given in the Old Testament, he held lightly all the extras that tradition had added to it. Some of these additions, such as the extraordinarily numerous and detailed Sabbath rules, angered him because they made life so burdensome for everybody. While people would have admitted that such extra rules were not in the Law, they were still part of the Jewish religion of the day. By criticizing them, Jesus became an enemy of the religious system.

- Jesus cared little about keeping those codes of social behaviour that had become part of everyday life. He befriended people who had been rejected by the religious teachers, such as tax collectors and prostitutes, and had meals with them. As if to underline the point that his acceptance of such people was not just for mealtimes, Jesus called a tax collector to be his disciple. Jesus' attitude to women – discussing religious issues with them, having them as followers and even teaching them – was also, no doubt, considered 'an affront to public decency'. It must have been easy to see Jesus as a dangerous revolutionary intent on undermining society. The Pharisees, who had firm ideas on how things ought to be run, clearly found Jesus particularly subversive.

- Jesus and his disciples seem to have lacked the perpetual seriousness that many people felt was an essential part of following God. When his disciples were accused of not fasting, Jesus' response to the criticism was revealing: 'For John the Baptist didn't drink wine and he often fasted, and you say, "He's demon possessed." And I, the Son of Man, feast and drink, and you say, "He's a glutton and a drunkard, and a friend of the worst sort of sinners!"'[29] In fact, to the Pharisees in particular, Jesus and his disciples must have appeared to be suspiciously lax in their behaviour: they were not religious enough!

- Although Jesus was careful to avoid making direct claims (at least in public) that he was either the Messiah or the Son of God until the end of his ministry, what he said and did strongly suggested that he viewed himself as more than a prophet. So, for instance, he maintained that he could forgive sins, something only God himself could do, and he claimed that God was his 'Father', which must have sounded blasphemous.

- Because Jesus claimed to bring – and to be – the fulfilment of all that Israel had been waiting for, he posed a challenge that had to be either accepted or rejected. Much of Jesus' teaching was either directly or indirectly critical of those who refused to accept him. So, when

Jesus talked about the new wine of his teaching needing new wineskins,[30] the implication that the faith of those who rejected him was a dry, old wineskin would hardly have been flattering.

- There were aspects to what Jesus taught that must have seemed unsettling or even heretical. Jesus' teachings put the centre of religious life not in keeping the Law, nor in offering sacrifices at the temple, but in being devoted to him personally. Claims such as these challenged the entire religious structure.

- There were hints in what Jesus said and did that implied the Gentiles could have a place in God's great scheme of things. This went against the widespread tone of national superiority that existed at the time. So, in Luke's account of Jesus teaching in the synagogue at Nazareth,[31] what angered the congregation was Jesus' reminder of how in the past, when God might have favoured his own people, he had instead dealt kindly with the Gentiles.

- Jesus posed a threat to the delicate balancing act that had been achieved between various power groups such as the Romans, the temple authorities and Herod. No doubt all the parties saw it as an imperfect arrangement, but with a nationalist uprising always a threat it was better than the alternative. These arrangements were not done out of a pure-minded desire to avoid bloodshed: there were strong financial incentives. The temple, in particular, provided very rich pickings: the historian Josephus[32] claimed that, at one Passover alone, the number of animal sacrifices offered was 256,500. Given that these animals had to be bought at the temple, such a figure suggests that it was a lucrative business. It is easy to imagine how someone with an investment in the temple system would have viewed anything – or anybody – that threatened the status quo. These shared concerns go some way to explain why, when it came to getting rid of Jesus, enemies were able to collaborate.

As is often the case, once the hostility began, it acquired its own momentum and soon found justification for its existence. So, once Jesus had been rejected as being a heretic, an explanation for his miracles had to be found. The obvious one was that he was doing them with demonic power,[33] something which gave his opponents another argument.*

There were also, no doubt, private and personal reasons why many people disliked Jesus. His moral standards were

---

* The accusation that Jesus' power was not divine but demonic outlasted his ministry. There are a number of Jewish references dating back to within a few centuries of Jesus' ministry that talk of him being a magician. In what is called the Babylonian Talmud (*Sanhedrin 107a*) there is a reference to 'Jesus the Nazarene who practised magic and led Israel astray'.

uncompromising, he challenged any sort of shallow superficial religion, he exposed hypocrisy and he asked for unconditional loyalty. Such reasons for rejecting Jesus are still with us.

Towards the end of this third phase of ministry, Jesus performed a miracle that pushed the hostility against him into something more organized and deadly. John's Gospel[34] records how Lazarus, one of Jesus' friends living at Bethany on the outskirts of Jerusalem, died and was buried. Four days after his death, Jesus visited his tomb and, in the presence of Lazarus' sisters and a crowd, ordered the removal of the stone that sealed the grave. He commanded that Lazarus come out and, still encumbered by his grave clothes, the man emerged. This was one of the most remarkable of all Jesus' miracles. It went far beyond mere resuscitation: after four days of burial, Lazarus' body would have undergone decay. Bethany's nearness to Jerusalem, the overwhelming nature of the miracle, and the fact that Lazarus was probably well known in Jerusalem meant that what had happened there was soon widely talked about. John tells us[35] that the ruling council – the Sanhedrin – met to discuss the matter and concluded that Jesus posed the threat of triggering a popular uprising that would provoke Roman retaliation. They resolved that Jesus be detained and executed.

On hearing the news that there was a warrant out for his arrest, Jesus went to a village near the wilderness until Passover.[36] The confrontation, when it came, would be at the time of his choosing, not theirs.

With the approach of Passover – the most politically charged of all the Jewish feasts – both Jesus' friends and enemies were waiting to see if he would turn up in Jerusalem. The remarkable miracle at Bethany had not been forgotten; indeed, much to the annoyance of Jesus' enemies, Lazarus had become something of a celebrity, a walking, talking testimony to Jesus' power.[37]

A week before the Passover feast began, Jesus and the disciples arrived in Bethany. There, probably on the Saturday night as the Sabbath ended,* a dinner was held in Jesus' honour with Lazarus present.[38] At the meal, Mary, one of Lazarus' sisters, anointed Jesus with an expensive ointment. Her action was critically received by the disciples and Jesus had to rebuke them; her action, he said, was a beautiful thing. Then he sounded an ominous note: what she had done was to anoint him for burial. Jesus was clearly in no doubt about what Jerusalem held in store for him.

All three accounts of this meal link with it the name of one disciple: Judas Iscariot. It seems that Judas – the treasurer of the Twelve – was especially aggrieved at what he saw as the frivolous waste of the valuable ointment. Soon afterwards he began discussions with Jesus' enemies in Jerusalem.

At this point, with Jesus just about to enter Jerusalem, we need to pause. All the pieces are now in place. In Jerusalem

---

* The Jewish day began and ended at sunset; so the Sabbath began on a Friday evening and ended on a Saturday at sunset.

and its outskirts we have Jesus, his puzzled followers, the would-be traitor, the excited crowds, the hostile Jewish leadership and the tense and nervous Roman authorities. The conflict looms.

Yet the events of the Last Week – the trial, crucifixion and resurrection – are so linked with the issues of what Jesus taught and who he claimed to be that these need to be examined first.

FOLLOWERS AND FRIENDS

One of the most important things that Jesus did was to call people to follow him. Those who obeyed that call included the twelve disciples, but there were many others as well.

Let's look at the Twelve first.

THE TWELVE

What does the word 'disciple' mean? To be a disciple is to be much more than a follower: you can 'follow' a football team and never leave the comfort of your settee. To be 'a disciple' carries with it ideas of dedication, obedience and effort. The best example of being a disciple would be the traditional picture of a person becoming apprenticed to a master in a particular craft or trade. To be a disciple of Jesus is to be an apprentice or imitator of him.

Jesus summoned Simon Peter and his brother Andrew from the middle of their work as fishermen and did the same with James and John; Matthew the tax collector had a similar unexpected call.[1] In these cases, the men responded by immediately leaving what they were doing and following Jesus. Eventually, Jesus had called twelve men to be with him.[2]

There are several striking features about the way that Jesus selected the disciples. The first, and perhaps the most striking, fact is that Jesus *called* them. While the religious teachers of the day also had disciples, they worked on a very different basis. In their case, it was the disciples who chose their teachers and not the other way round. A young man who wanted religious instruction would have looked at the rabbis on offer, chosen the one that he felt was the best instructor of the Law, and then applied to become one of his pupils. Doing what Jesus did, choosing and summoning people to follow him *personally*, was as rare then as it is now.

Secondly, the focus of the discipleship that Jesus called the men to was unusual. To follow a rabbi was to learn from him how to study God's Law. Yet Mark says: 'Jesus went up on a mountain and called the ones he wanted to go with him. And they came to him. Then he selected twelve of them to be his regular companions . . .'[3] Jesus was calling the disciples not to study the Law but to be *with him*. By doing that, Jesus put himself above the Law.

Thirdly, by choosing to call twelve men, Jesus was doing something symbolic. Since its earliest days, the nation of Israel had been made up of twelve tribes and the loss of most of these tribes nearly eight hundred years earlier into Assyrian captivity had been a body blow to the Jewish faith. One of the promises associated with the coming Messiah was that he would restore the nation of Israel and the missing tribes.[4] By choosing twelve followers, Jesus was claiming to be the one who would restore and remake God's people.*

WHY DID JESUS HAVE DISCIPLES?

There were other reasons why Jesus called the Twelve:

They were to be his witnesses

Jesus had disciples so that they would act as witnesses to who he was. They were to be people who could say that they knew him and could testify to what he had done. Turning the Twelve into effective witnesses involved two things: teaching them and sending them.

Jesus taught his followers both directly and indirectly. In the gospels, we see Jesus directly instructing the Twelve in private, explaining his parables to them and asking them questions to make them think. Indirect learning was also important in the training of the Twelve: Jesus kept them close to him for what

---

* The fact that the number twelve was so important explains why, after Judas' betrayal and suicide, the remaining disciples made it an urgent priority to appoint a replacement for him (Acts 1:15–26).

was in all probability the best part of three years and the influence of that must have been enormous. Much of what the Twelve learned must have been caught, not taught.

We see that early on in their discipleship, Jesus sent the disciples out to be witnesses for him. As part of that task, he gave them his authority. The Twelve thus became his authorized representatives: they stood in his place. To accept one of the Twelve was to accept Jesus; to reject one was to reject him.*

With the resurrection and the coming of the Holy Spirit, the role of witness acquired a new depth and breadth. The depth lay in the fact that Jesus' disciples were now to be those who could testify that he had risen from the dead. The breadth lay in the way that they were to take that message to the whole world.[5]

They were to help him

One important role of a disciple was to give Jesus practical help. Much of what the Twelve did was routine and unspectacular: they tried to manage the crowds around Jesus, were responsible for getting food and were in charge of making arrangements.[6]

It would be misleading, however, to see the disciples' help as being only practical. There is no reason to doubt that Jesus had

---

* The word 'apostle' carries the idea of someone being an authorised delegate or agent.

the universal human need for friendship and community. The Twelve – and the others – were not just Jesus' followers, they were also his friends.

They were to be the basis of a new community

Jesus chose the Twelve not just to be a dozen individuals but to be the beginning of a new people, a restored or recreated Israel built around himself. In fact, much of Jesus' teaching to them was about how this new community was to function. So we see him teaching his followers that they are to be humble, to be forgiving, to show sacrificial love and to be servants of one another. So tightly-knit and caring is this new community that it is more a family than an organization. In fact, when Jesus talks about his disciples after the resurrection, he calls them 'my brothers'.[7]

A PROFILE OF THE TWELVE

From the four lists in the New Testament[8] we can see that the Twelve were: Simon Peter, Andrew, James, John, Philip, Bartholomew (or Nathaniel), Matthew, Thomas, James the Less, Judas, the son of Jacob (or Thaddeus), Simon the Zealot and Judas Iscariot. Although many varied and interesting traditions exist concerning all of the Twelve, hard facts about them are few. Indeed, for almost half we know virtually nothing.

Simon Peter and Andrew were fishermen brothers who had been followers of John the Baptist. *Simon Peter*, who had originally been called Simon before Jesus changed his name to Peter ('the Rock'), was the spokesperson for the Twelve from the start. In the gospels, Peter's record as a disciple is uneven. The high point was his declaration that he believed Jesus was the Messiah; his low point came during the trial of Jesus when he repeatedly denied that he ever knew him. After the resurrected Jesus had restored him to fellowship and the Spirit had been given, Peter became leader of the early church. We know that Peter was married and that he took his wife with him on his later travels.[9] We know much less about his brother *Andrew*.

James and *John*, the sons of Zebedee, were another pair of fishermen. Jesus termed the two 'the sons of thunder',[10] possibly because of their volatile tempers. About *Philip* and *Bartholomew* we know very little. From the parallel accounts of the conversion of *Matthew*, we know that he was also known as Levi. Originally a tax collector, *Matthew* is considered the author of the first gospel.

Thomas has, perhaps unfairly, become notorious for his doubts about the resurrection of Jesus.[11] This has overshadowed his earlier determination to follow Jesus regardless of the cost and his extraordinary insight in recognizing the resurrected Jesus as Lord and God.[12]

Of *James the Less* we know little. It is generally assumed that the 'Mary the mother of James and Joseph' who was at the crucifixion and the discovery of the empty tomb was his mother.[13] In this case, a disciple's mother is more notable than he is!

Judas the son of Jacob is another obscure figure, who also went under the name of Thaddeus. It seems likely that *Simon the Zealot* was so called because he had held militant revolutionary views.

On account of his betrayal of Jesus, *Judas Iscariot* is a name that always comes at the end of all the lists of the Twelve. Judas was the treasurer for Jesus and the disciples.

While we do not know why Jesus chose the men that he did, two features stand out. One is that all the Twelve seem to have been ordinary working men without any formal religious training.[14] The other is that the Twelve were a diverse group, drawn from many differing backgrounds and professions. This diversity was probably deliberate and part of Jesus' vision of creating a new people of God.*

We know little about what ultimately happened to most of the Twelve. James was executed by Herod Agrippa sometime before AD 44 and so became the first of the Twelve to be

---

* Sceptics tend to see Jesus as a wandering preacher with a short-term agenda who would have been astonished by the church that grew up in his name. Yet the way Jesus laboured to teach and train the Twelve suggests that he intended to create a movement that would last and spread.

martyred.[15] The traditions that tell of Peter being martyred in Rome around AD 64 are probably correct. Other traditions that speak of John living to an old age in Ephesus and being the only one of the Twelve not to be martyred are believable. There is good evidence that the tales that Thomas went as far as India to preach are true.* But about the rest there are only legends. What we do know, though, is that the apostles took their mission to preach the good news of Jesus to the ends of the earth seriously. It may not be too far-fetched to imagine them sitting down around the best map of the known world and deciding who would go where. Certainly, within a few years of the resurrection, most of the Twelve seem to have left Jerusalem. The fact that by AD 100 there were flourishing churches across most of the known world is proof that most of the Twelve did the job they were trained for.

OTHER FOLLOWERS

Jesus had a much larger group of followers who were also considered 'disciples': on one occasion, he sent out a group of seventy-two who were known as such.[16] These other disciples also put themselves under Jesus' authority and obeyed his teaching. Yet there were differences:

* To this day there are 'Mar Toma' ('Saint Thomas') churches in India that claim Thomas as their founder.

- Whereas the Twelve were called, at least some of this group had chosen to follow Jesus.[17]
- The larger group included women.
- The larger group of disciples was very varied socially. Some were well off. One of the women was Joanna, 'the wife of Chuza, Herod's business manager' and she and many other women used their own resources to support Jesus and his disciples.[18] Others were from lower down the social ladder. The extent of these social extremes is seen in the two people who became followers of Jesus in Jericho: Bartimaeus, a beggar whose sight had been restored, and Zacchaeus, a chief tax collector.[19]
- The larger group of disciples was not restricted to one age bracket. We know that at least three mothers followed Jesus at least some of the time: Mary, the mother of Jesus; the mother of James and John, and the mother of James. Jesus' mother must have been close to fifty and the other two were at least forty. That may not seem striking until you realize that then, if you survived the first few years of childhood, your life expectancy was around forty years[20] rather than our seventy-plus years. In other words, these women were the equivalent of our senior citizens.
- Some of the people in this larger group do not appear to have left their homes or jobs. So Lazarus, Mary and Martha stayed in Bethany. John describes Joseph of

Arimathea, a rich member of the Sanhedrin, as a secret disciple of Jesus.[21]

Two points arise from this larger group. First, they were not, in any way, 'second-class' disciples. It was the women of this group who stood by Jesus at the cross and many of the resurrection appearances were to those in this group: the women, Cleopas and his companion, the 'more than five hundred' that Paul refers to.[22] Second, it is this larger and more varied group of followers, not the Twelve, who provide us with a model for who should constitute the church.

! JESUS AND WOMEN

The presence of women in the larger group of Jesus' followers raises the issue of Jesus and women.

In the culture of Jesus' time, as in most of the ancient world, the role of women was largely limited to being home-based wives and mothers. Although Jewish culture was much more pro-women than most other societies of the time, women were still treated as little more than possessions. Josephus, despite being a well-educated Jew, managed to claim that it was the teaching of 'Scripture' that 'a woman is inferior to her husband in all things'.[23] (What 'Scripture' Josephus believed he was quoting is unknown; it certainly wasn't the Old Testament.) That such negative values were widely held can be seen in the disciples' surprised response to finding Jesus talking with a woman in Samaria.[24]

Jesus, however, was radical in his views on women:

- Jesus' followers included various women, some of whom travelled with him and the Twelve. For any man to travel with such a female entourage in such a culture was – and is – almost unknown.

- Women played a major role in the events of Easter week. The only followers who stayed with Jesus at the cross, apart from John the disciple, were women.

- Women are prominent in the accounts of the resurrection. In particular, the risen Jesus appeared first to Mary Magdalene and instructed her 'to go and tell his brothers'. The first witness of the resurrection was a woman.[25]

- Jesus taught women, evidently with the view that they could, in turn, teach. When Luke tells us that Mary 'sat at Jesus' feet listening to his word' he is using the technical expression for a student being taught by a rabbi.[26]

- Jesus defended women. When presented with a woman 'caught in adultery' Jesus refused to condemn her and, after forcing her male accusers to leave, let her go with a warning.[27]

- In the culture of the day, women were considered the source of sexual sin. Yet in the Sermon on the Mount, Jesus blames men, not women, for lust.[28]

- In his parables, Jesus makes almost equal use of images from the worlds of women and men and uses women as positive models. So, for example, in one parable about a woman who searches for a lost coin, the woman represents God.[29]

- The longest discussion recorded in the gospels is between Jesus and the woman of Samaria.[30]

- Jesus' teaching on divorce is revealing. In the culture of the day, a man saw his wife as little more than property and divorce was easy. So Josephus could write: 'At this period I divorced my wife, being displeased at her behaviour.'[31] If a man did divorce his wife, any hurt or insult was considered done to the woman's family, not to her. Yet Jesus taught: 'Whoever divorces his wife and marries someone else commits adultery against her.'[32]

In a world that saw women as pieces of property whose role was to be submissive to men, Jesus saw them as genuine human beings of equal worth and dignity.

MIRACLES

The four gospels describe Jesus performing around thirty-six specific miracles and mention that he did many more. The miracles are of different types.

Jesus healed people: he is described as restoring sight,[1] healing contagious skin disorders,[2] healing the lame,[3] curing fevers,[4] putting back a severed ear,[5] stopping a haemorrhage[6] and restoring a withered hand.[7] The most extreme form of healing is provided by three records of Jesus bringing people back to life:* Jairus' daughter, a widow's son and Lazarus of Bethany.[8]

Jesus had an extraordinary power over nature: he miraculously multiplied bread and fish,[9] changed water into wine,[10] calmed a storm,[11] walked on water[12] and gave fishermen

---

* These were different from Jesus' own resurrection. That involved his body being transformed into a radically new form that would never die again. These were 'merely' reanimations and the people involved eventually died again.

miraculous catches of fish.[13] Jesus had miraculous knowledge and was aware of hidden facts and attitudes.[14] Jesus also performed exorcisms of people oppressed by demonic powers.[15]

The way in which Jesus did miracles is distinctive:

- Jesus often performed miracles in a quiet and unspectacular way. Sometimes he turned bystanders away in order to perform miracles; on other occasions he asked that his healings not be reported.[16] There was nothing of the showman about Jesus.
- Jesus performed miracles with the minimum of actions and words, generally healing with no more than a few words and sometimes a gesture.[17]
- The basis of Jesus' miracles was his own personal authority. He is never recorded as praying for God to do a miracle, or even doing a miracle in God's name: he did them himself.
- Jesus refused to do miracles on demand to prove who he was and he had little time for sensation seekers.[18] He never did miracles for profit or publicity or even to save himself.[19] Jesus' motive in doing miracles is given as compassion.[20]

! THE MYTH OF THE MIRACLE-FREE JESUS

Over the last two hundred years, there have been countless attempts to explain away Jesus' miracles as misinterpretations, hallucinations or myths created later. Some attempts border on the ridiculous: as when Jesus' walking on water is explained away as the disciples' failure to notice that he was really strolling at the water's edge. Others assume that Palestine was entirely populated by people ready to cry 'miracle!' at the slightest coincidence.

In reality, it is hard to create a 'miracle-free' Jesus. The 'supernatural' is present throughout the gospels, not just in the miracles but in the virginal conception, in appearances of angels and in prophecies. It is not even easy to imagine the development of the gospels from some miracle-free source: Mark – the earliest gospel – has more miracles per page than the others.

The miracles are also so tightly interwoven with Jesus' teaching and the events of his life that it is hard to remove them. For instance, the gospels record a major crisis when, just after Jesus had miraculously fed five thousand men and their families, the crowd wanted to make him king.[21] To propose there was no miracle makes nonsense of the account: it is hard to see how thousands of people sharing their packed lunches together would have generated the enthusiasm to declare Jesus king!

Equally, the rest of the New Testament assumes that Jesus did miracles. In Acts, for instance, Peter says this of Jesus: 'People of Israel, listen! God publicly endorsed Jesus of Nazareth by doing wonderful miracles, wonders, and signs through him, as you well know.'[22]

Finally, but importantly, the few traditions about Jesus outside the New Testament talk about him as an exorcist and a miracle worker.* None of the hostile references to Jesus deny his miracles; they simply consider them as being due to him having occult power.[23]

In summary, you cannot remove the miraculous from the life of Jesus; it runs through the accounts of his life like the lettering in a stick of rock and it is just as hard to remove. Either we accept that Jesus is an almost entirely invented figure or we somehow accept the miraculous in the gospels. There is no halfway house.

---

* Early in the fourth century, the historian Eusebius described how a man called Quadratus had written to the Emperor Hadrian in around AD 120, defending Christianity. The full text of what Quadratus wrote is lost, but Eusebius quotes a long sentence from it in his *Ecclesiastical Histories* (IV.3): 'The works of our Saviour were lasting, for they were genuine: those who were healed and those who were raised from the dead were seen not only when they were healed and when they were raised but were also present, not merely while the Saviour was on earth, but also after his death; they were alive for quite a while, so that some of them lived even to our day.' In other words, some of those raised from the dead and healed by Jesus around AD 30 were still alive around the end of the first century as witnesses to his power.

Jesus' Miracles: Do they Make Sense?

Many people assume as a basic principle of life that 'all miracles are impossible', and so when they come to the subject of Jesus' miracles they are forced to conclude that, however authentic these accounts may seem, they simply *cannot* be true.

But *are* miracles impossible?

Denial is a minority opinion

To deny the possibility of the miraculous is to hold to a minority opinion. Almost all cultures that have ever existed have believed in some sort of God (or gods), that prayer works and that there are supernatural forces of good and evil. Atheism has been largely confined to some people in Western culture from the late nineteenth century onwards. Even here, such scepticism is only skin-deep, as is evidenced by the astonishing hunger for books and films based on the supernatural or magic. Of course, the majority can be wrong, but the scarcity of cultures based on a total scepticism about the miraculous is very striking.

Nature does not prohibit miracles

There is no fundamental reason for ruling out the possibility of miracles. Although you often hear people say things like 'the Laws of Nature prohibit miracles', such statements betray a misunderstanding of what these laws are about. What scientists call 'laws' are simply a provisional description of those principles by which the universe has been observed to work. They do not – and cannot – rule out the possibility of those principles changing. In the Bible, God is described as the one who keeps every part of the universe going, whether it is in the big things like the rising of the sun or in the tiny things like the growth of a plant. So any 'Laws of Nature' are simply a record of how God normally works and, as the being who both made the universe and keeps it going, God has a perfect right to do something different. On that basis, any Laws of Nature can only *describe* what has been seen to happen; they cannot *prescribe* what must happen. In the fifth century Saint Augustine wrote, 'Miracles are not contrary to nature; but only contrary to what we know about nature.'

Knowledge is limited

To say that miracles *cannot* occur is to claim that you completely understand how the universe works. If it were possible to put the universe on a laboratory bench and examine it, then such a claim would make better sense. The possibility that there might be something – or someone – *outside* the physical universe is something that we can neither prove nor disprove.

The impossibility of miracles is unproven

Much of the scepticism about miracles derives from the sort of confident scientific view of the universe that prevailed before

Einstein. Ever since the Theory of Relativity the universe has become so much stranger that it is hard to be dogmatic about the impossibility of miracles. Very strange things occur in quantum physics.* They don't prove that miracles do occur, but they do suggest that you should be very cautious about saying that they can't happen. It is not, generally speaking, scientists who say that science proves that miracles are impossible: they know better.

The evidence of healing

One of the most discussed areas of the miraculous is that of healing. Most Christians would probably have personal experience of at least one case where, in answer to prayer, there has been a healing that defied all natural explanation. Many could recount numerous such experiences.[24] The issues here are complex: was the original diagnosis correct? Was there a purely psychological effect? Nevertheless, even when you disregard any case that is even remotely questionable, numerous cases of apparently miraculous healings remain.[25]

---

* A spectacular example is what is called 'quantum entanglement' which seems to (and possibly does) break the law of cause and effect. Here two particles of light can be so interlinked that, even if separated by millions of miles, a change in one particle will instantaneously affect the other without there being *any connection whatever between them*. The whole thing so unnerved Einstein that he called it 'spooky action at a distance'.

To say all these things is not to defend every claimed case of the paranormal. It is to point out that if Jesus was indeed God become one of us, there is a perfect logic in him performing miracles. As 'the Word',[26] the universe's maker, Jesus had both the authority and the power to do what he chose with his creation. For such a unique person to perform unique acts makes sense.

THE MEANING OF JESUS' MIRACLES

Why did Jesus perform miracles? He didn't do them for fame or fortune, or even as a means to gather crowds. John's Gospel gives us a clue: they are 'signs'. The miracles are signposts that, for those who consider them carefully, point to the truth. Five particular truths stand out.

Jesus' miracles point to his identity

The fact that Jesus did miracles showed that he was, at least, a prophet. The greatest miracle workers of the Old Testament were all prophets: Moses, Elijah and Elisha. Indeed, some of Jesus' miracles carry unmistakable echoes of all three. Moses oversaw the miraculous feeding of vast crowds in the wilderness; Jesus did the same.[27] Elijah brought a widow's son back to life; so did Jesus.[28] Elisha healed a leper; Jesus heals ten.[29] Many of those who considered Jesus' actions concluded from them that he was a prophet.[30] The miracles demonstrated that Jesus was God's approved messenger and that God was with him.[31]

The miracles also pointed deeper: by showing that Jesus had the power over sin and evil that was expected of God's King, they pointed to him being the Messiah. When answering John the Baptist's enquiry as to whether he was the Messiah, Jesus gave this answer to John's followers: 'Tell him about what you have heard and seen – the blind see, the lame walk, the lepers are cured, the deaf hear, the dead are raised to life, and the Good News is being preached to the poor.'[32] In the three miracles involving raising the dead, Jesus demonstrated that he was Lord over death itself.

The miracles also pointed to Jesus being more than any man. Mark tells us that after Jesus had calmed a storm, the disciples 'were filled with awe and said among themselves, "Who is this man, that even the wind and waves obey him?"'[33] They knew the Old Testament saw the stilling of storms as something that only God could do.[34] And when Jesus walked on water, they declared that he was 'the Son of God' for the same reason.[35] Jesus also used a miracle of healing to show he could forgive sins: another action that only God could do.[36]

Jesus' miracles pointed to the fact that he was not only a prophet but also the Messiah, the king of Israel. Yet they went beyond even that: by doing what only God could do, Jesus showed he was the divine Son of God.

Jesus' miracles point to the coming of God's kingdom

The gospel writers link Jesus' miracles to the coming of God's kingdom. As God's king, Jesus began to bring God's rule of peace and justice into a turbulent world that had rebelled against him. This aspect of the miracles is most dramatically seen in the encounters that Jesus had with occult powers.[37] When criticized for exorcizing a demonized man, Jesus said: 'But if I am casting out demons by the power of God, then the Kingdom of God has arrived among you.'[38] Jesus was God's king who fought Satan's forces and as he extended God's kingdom, he liberated captives.[39]

Most people in the West today have little experience of the demonic and many find the reports of exorcisms in the gospels problematic. Some people have tried to rationalize such accounts; explaining them away as illnesses and psychological disturbances that Jesus, as a man of his time, saw as demonic. Yet several facts must be considered. First, Jesus clearly distinguished between illness and demonic possession. So, for instance, while Jesus often touched the sick as part of his healing, he never laid hands on demoniacs but instead simply issued an order for the evil spirit to depart. Second, the apparent absence of such phenomena in the West may be misleading. In parts of the world where occult practices, including the worship of spirits, are widespread, demonic phenomena and possession appear to be common. Third, possession and demonic phenomena seem to be more common at some times and places than at others. Many authors have seen the apparent epidemic of open demonic activity at the time of Jesus as a sign of the unparalleled warfare then taking place between Jesus and Satan.

Jesus' teaching centred on God's kingdom and it is helpful to remember the Kingdom is not a matter of words or concepts, but about a spiritual struggle with the human race's great enemy, the devil. Jesus' miracles demonstrated that he was the victor in this struggle.

Jesus' miracles point to God's coming reign

Miracles also point to the future. They look forward to the day when, at Jesus' return, God's kingdom will be fully established. They are like cinema trailers showing something of the forthcoming attraction: the ultimate restoration of the universe. So the healing of the sick looks forward to the time when there will be no illness, the raising of the dead to the ending of death itself, the feeding of the crowds to the great banquet of eternity.[40]

Jesus' miracles point to God's character

Jesus' miracles don't just show us that he is the Messiah; they show us what kind of Messiah he is. In the miracles we see something of Jesus' compassion and mercy. Even at the moment of his arrest, when Jesus might have been fully justified in thinking of himself, he showed his compassion by healing one of his enemies.[41] In the Old Testament, God describes himself as compassionate and merciful: Jesus' miracles demonstrated what that means in practice.[42]

Particularly significant is the fact that the gospels record Jesus performing miracles for people at the edges of society: a woman with a condition that left her ritually unclean, blind beggars, ostracized lepers and demoniacs expelled from their community. Jesus didn't just heal Jews either: he healed Samaritans and Gentiles too.

Jesus' miracles show us something of God's heart towards the human race and the world he has made.

Jesus' miracles point to the need to have faith in him

At the end of his gospel, John wrote this: 'Jesus' disciples saw him do many other miraculous signs besides the ones recorded in this book. But these are written so that you may believe that Jesus is the Messiah, the Son of God, and that by believing in him you will have life.'[43]

Jesus' miracles are events that require a response. They are not curiosities of history to be debated or paranormal phenomena to be analysed; they are calls to commitment. They are encouragements to those who have no faith to look deeper and they are invitations to those on the edge of faith to come on and take the final step.

Yet it is important to note that while miracles can generate faith, they do not compel it. How you treat a miracle depends on what you believe; faith is required in order to understand correctly the significance of the miracles. So, in Jesus' time, there were many people who saw his miracles but denied their meaning. Some, no doubt, thought they had seen an illusion, others that they had merely witnessed some bizarre marvel of nature. Still others saw the miracles as coming from the devil. [44]

Miracles, however, should never be dismissed carelessly. The gospels make it clear that to reject the evidence of a miracle is a serious matter. Jesus gave the following sad warning over two towns in which he had done miracles: 'What horrors await you, Korazin and Bethsaida! For if the miracles I did in you had been done in wicked Tyre and Sidon, their people would have sat in deep repentance long ago, clothed in sackcloth and throwing ashes on their heads to show their remorse.'[45]

Jesus' miracles are best seen as signs. For those who are prepared to think about them, they point to many things: who Jesus is, the character of his kingdom, the nature of the future and God's character. Above all, Jesus' miracles challenged people to give their verdict on him.

They still do.

How Jesus Taught

Jesus sometimes referred to himself as 'the Teacher'[1] and his reputation as a teacher (a 'rabbi') was such that large crowds travelled long distances to hear him.

Jesus' teaching style was rooted in the Jewish tradition but, despite some similarities, it was different to that of his contemporaries. When the temple guards were sent to arrest Jesus, they returned empty-handed to the authorities with the excuse 'We have never heard anyone talk like this!'[2]

While the rabbis expected people to come to them, Jesus went out to the people. He taught not only in synagogues and in the temple but also in homes, in fields, while travelling and even from a boat. And while the rabbis tended to teach only a select group of male disciples, Jesus taught everybody. He had his own disciples but he also taught people that the rabbis considered unworthy of teaching: women, children, tax collectors, 'sinners' and even Samaritans and Gentiles.

Jesus taught wherever and whenever he could; he spoke to large crowds and to individuals. Sometimes he chose the topics, while on other occasions he let some incident or encounter act as a springboard for a lesson. Whether it was news of an atrocity or the blessing of babies, Jesus could use it as the basis for teaching.[3]

Jesus was a skilful communicator. He used many different ways of communicating: riddles, puns, proverbs and, above all, vivid imagery. Jesus was a great master of the most difficult thing in any language – saying everything in a handful of words:

- 'Do for others what you would like them to do for you. This is a summary of all that is taught in the law and the prophets.'[4]
- 'You are not defiled by what you eat; you are defiled by what you say and do!'[5]
- 'The Sabbath was made to benefit people, and not people to benefit the Sabbath.'[6]
- 'Real life is not measured by how much we own.'[7]

Jesus often used irony and paradox to turn prevailing wisdom upside down:

- 'God blesses those who realize their need for him, for the Kingdom of Heaven is given to them. God blesses those who mourn, for they will be comforted.'[8]

137

- 'If you refuse to take up your cross and follow me, you are not worthy of being mine. If you cling to your life, you will lose it; but if you give it up for me, you will find it.'[9]
- 'But among you, those who are the greatest should take the lowest rank, and the leader should be like a servant.'[10]

Of course, this wasn't just wordplay; it reflected the fact that the Kingdom really did turn everything upside down. And Jesus didn't just say things in an extraordinary way: he said extraordinary things too. Both his content and his presentation were remarkable.

Whether his hearers were hostile or hurting, Jesus always seems to have known what to say. On one occasion, he was asked whether it was right to pay taxes to the Romans. It was the trickiest of questions: to say 'no' was to ask to be arrested by the Romans; to say 'yes' was to guarantee the loss of popular support. Jesus' answer was 'Give to Caesar what belongs to him. But everything that belongs to God must be given to God.'[11] Jesus' answer, unsurpassed after two thousand years, converts a challenge to him into one for his hearers.

One of the key elements in Jesus' teaching was his use of stories and illustrations – what have become known as 'parables'. We rarely use parables in our contemporary Western world, so it is worth looking at them more closely.

THE PARABLES

Let's look at three examples of parables:

The mustard seed

Jesus asked, 'How can I describe the Kingdom of God? What story should I use to illustrate it? It is like a tiny mustard seed. Though this is one of the smallest of seeds, it grows to become one of the largest of plants, with long branches where birds can come and find shelter.'[12]

In this parable, barely a sentence long, Jesus says that God's kingdom has not come in visible glory but instead as something small and humble that can easily be overlooked. Nevertheless, like the mustard seed, the Kingdom will grow and extend until birds can shelter in it. Those of Jesus' hearers who knew their Scriptures well might have remembered that there it was the Gentiles who were pictured as 'birds'.[13] The Kingdom, Jesus is hinting, will one day expand beyond Israel.

The Pharisee and the tax collector

Then Jesus told this story to some who had great self-confidence and scorned everyone else: 'Two men went to the temple to pray. One was a Pharisee, and the other was a dishonest tax collector. The proud Pharisee stood by himself and prayed this prayer: "I thank you, God, that I am not a sinner like everyone else, especially like that tax collector over there! For I never cheat, I don't sin, I don't commit adultery, I fast twice a week, and I give you a tenth of my income."

'But the tax collector stood at a distance and dared not even lift his eyes to heaven as he prayed. Instead, he beat his chest in sorrow, saying, "O God, be merciful to me, for I am a sinner." I tell you, this sinner, not the Pharisee, returned home justified before God. For the proud will be humbled, but the humble will be honoured.'[14]

This was one of the problems of Jesus' day: many Jewish people felt that because they kept the Law (or thought they did) they were right with God. They had become complacent.

When he announced that his story was about a Pharisee and a tax collector, Jesus' hearers would have known what to expect. They would have known the Pharisee was going to be the hero as these were the only people who fully kept the Law. They would have known, too, that the tax collector didn't have a hope. Tax collectors were not just crooks: they were politically condemned because they worked for Rome and spiritually condemned because their contact with the Gentiles made them unclean. So when the two went to the temple it was a no-contest situation.

Jesus' reversal of everyone's expectations in his story must have caused astonishment and outrage. But those of his hearers who knew that they could never meet the standards of the

Pharisees must have found enormous encouragement in the idea that God hears and forgives those who are repentant.

The parable of the lost son

This story, often known as the parable of the prodigal son (to be *prodigal* is to be recklessly wasteful) is the third in a sequence about the finding of lost things.[15] The background to this parable is that the Pharisees were complaining that Jesus was associating with 'sinners',[16] and the story is part of Jesus' reply to them.

'A man had two sons. The younger son told his father, "I want my share of your estate now, instead of waiting until you die." So his father agreed to divide his wealth between his sons.

'A few days later this younger son packed all his belongings and took a trip to a distant land, and there he wasted all his money on wild living. About the time his money ran out, a great famine swept over the land, and he began to starve. He persuaded a local farmer to hire him to feed his pigs. The boy became so hungry that even the pods he was feeding the pigs looked good to him. But no one gave him anything.

'When he finally came to his senses, he said to himself, "At home even the hired men have food enough to spare, and here I am, dying of hunger! I will go home to my father and say, 'Father, I have sinned against both heaven and you, and I am no longer worthy of being called your son. Please take me on as a hired man.'"

'So he returned home to his father. And while he was still a long distance away, his father saw him coming. Filled with love and compassion, he ran to his son, embraced him, and kissed him. His son said to him, "Father, I have sinned against both heaven and you, and I am no longer worthy of being called your son."

'But his father said to the servants, "Quick! Bring the finest robe in the house and put it on him. Get a ring for his finger, and sandals for his feet. And kill the calf we have been fattening in the pen. We must celebrate with a feast, for this son of mine was dead and has now returned to life. He was lost, but now he is found." So the party began.

'Meanwhile, the older son was in the fields working. When he returned home, he heard music and dancing in the house, and he asked one of the servants what was going on. "Your brother is back," he was told, "and your father has killed the calf we were fattening and has prepared a great feast. We are celebrating because of his safe return."

'The older brother was angry and wouldn't go in. His father came out and begged him, but he replied, "All these years I've worked hard for you and never once refused to do a single thing you told me to. And in all that time you never gave me even one young goat for a feast with my friends. Yet when this son of yours comes back after squandering your money on prostitutes, you celebrate by killing the finest calf we have."

'His father said to him, "Look, dear son, you and I are very close, and everything I have is yours. We had to celebrate this happy day. For your brother was dead and has come back to life! He was lost, but now he is found!"' [17]

The parable deals with familiar and universal characters (the young rebel, the good father, the loyal older son), yet it deals with them in an unexpected way. The shocking nature of the younger son's request mustn't be overlooked. To ask for your inheritance *before* your father died was a shameful act of disrespect that said, in effect, 'I wish you were dead.' Jesus' hearers would have felt that for such a son to be reduced to the unspeakable horrors of eating with pigs among the Gentiles was a well-deserved punishment.

Yet it is here the plot takes its first surprising swing. The son decides to return home and ask to be a servant. You can imagine Jesus' listeners wondering about the ethics of this: the son deserved judgement, not the mercy of being given a job. Surely, the father would have to refuse?

As the young man returns home, however, there is a further twist, one that must have turned the bemused looks into startled frowns. The father, waiting in expectation, sees the son coming: 'Filled with love and compassion, he ran to his son, embraced him, and kissed him.' In this culture, no one with any honour ever runs: it is too shameful. By running and – still worse – by embracing the rebel, the father shames himself and sacrifices his dignity and his honour. Even more shocking is the way that the father, overflowing with lavish love, refuses to hear the son's request to be treated as a servant but instead reinstates him publicly as his son.

Yet just at the point when you expect universal celebration and 'they all lived happily ever after', the story takes another remarkable turn. The older son, who by staying at home must have seemed the hero of the story, is now shown to be embittered and sour. His refusal to join in the celebrations means that he insults the father. His father's generous love to his brother has so angered him that he is revealed as a rebel. The son who was lost has been found but the son who did not realize he was lost remains lost.

The message of the parable of the lost son is that God, as a loving father, is prepared to make a sacrifice to accept back the lost who return to him in repentance. But those who object, like some of Jesus' original hearers, to the warm welcome given to the lost who return show that they know nothing of the Father and his love: they do not realize that they are lost themselves.

THINKING ABOUT THE PARABLES

So what is a parable? It is sometimes a story, but can be just an illustration or an image. In fact, perhaps the simplest and most useful definition of a parable is that it is 'an indirect way of speaking'. The English word *parabola*, which describes a type of curved path or orbit, helps us: you can consider parables as 'verbal parabolas', a 'curved way' of speaking.

The images of Jesus' parables are revealing. They are all based on the ordinary and familiar worlds of the people who heard him speak; they are pictures of fields, feasts and families.* The images are strong enough to catch the attention but never so strong that they overwhelm the message.

Jesus' extensive use of parables was distinctive. Even Jesus' disciples were puzzled at how much use he made of parables.[18] So why did he use them? There are several reasons.

One reason is that *parables are memorable*. It is well known that a story or an image lingers in the mind longer than a statement: that's why companies have trademarks and logos. By anchoring his message in images, Jesus was ensuring that it could be easily remembered and repeated.

Another reason is that *parables get around defences*. If Jesus had announced that he was going to speak on 'the evil of not

---

* Some people consider that Jesus' teaching was actually invented by the early church. In fact, the images and language used in the parables confirm their authenticity. In Jesus' teaching, there is no trace of the urban Greco-Roman world that was the base of the early church; instead we encounter a world that is largely rural, firmly Jewish and completely Palestinian. The early Christians transmitted Jesus' teaching; they didn't create it.

welcoming repentant sinners', no doubt many of his hearers would have stopped listening, especially if they knew that they were being targeted. Instead, Jesus told them such stories as 'The Lost Son' and by the time they had recognized what he was saying, it was too late: the message had penetrated. The parabola image is helpful here: like a skilfully spun cricket ball, the good parable curves in past defences to strike its target.

Still another reason is that *parables invite a response*. To teach facts alone is to ask for nothing more demanding than memorization. Parables, though, go much deeper: by inviting us to identify with the characters they provoke us into making a response.

Yet Jesus used parables for still other reasons. Mark says that Jesus 'used many such stories and illustrations to teach the people as much as they were able to understand. In fact, in his public teaching he taught only with parables, but afterwards when he was alone with his disciples, he explained the meaning to them.'[19] In other words, Jesus used parables when talking to outsiders, but not to the Twelve. Why?

Firstly, parables allow *indirect confrontation*. In most traditional societies there is a great deal of sensitivity to shame and honour, and the modern Western habit of going 'straight to the point' is just too abrupt. In such societies, parables are common because they provide a way of saying unpopular things without inflicting public shame. Even today, anyone working in the Middle East or Asia soon learns to pay careful attention to any stories they are told, just in case they conceal a hidden message. So, for instance, rather than directly criticizing an employee in public for being late, a manager might instead tell a story about how once, some late-arriving employee had had their salary cut. The person targeted by the parable would recognize the warning. At times, Jesus used parables precisely for this reason. So rather than directly attack the self-righteous Pharisees, Jesus told the stories of 'The Pharisee and the Tax Collector' and 'The Lost Son'.*

Secondly, parables give the *protection of ambiguity*. Because they are an indirect means of communication, they can provide a way of making a challenging statement without stirring up trouble. On some occasions, Jesus' parables serve just such a role. After all, the Kingdom of God was a dangerous topic and Jesus had many enemies. Think, for instance, of rephrasing the parable of the mustard seed into a statement: 'the Kingdom will grow until it extends over the whole world and the Gentiles are part of it.' Hearing it put like that, the Jewish religious authorities would have been scandalized and the Romans would have been alarmed. But expressed as a parable it was different. Those who had 'tuned in' to what Jesus was saying would have understood what was meant; anyone else would have found it just too enigmatic.

---

* Eventually Jesus did make direct attacks on such people (see Matthew 23); clearly the subtle message of the parables had been ignored.

Thirdly, parables *separate seekers from the merely curious*. Jesus was seeking people who would be prepared to be his disciples: he was looking for commitment, not curiosity. Here, parables acted as the great filtering mechanism for his audiences. They produced two reactions. Some people would have heard the stories and then walked away feeling no more than entertained or slightly puzzled. Others would have found themselves compelled and intrigued by what they heard and might have sought Jesus afterwards, saying, 'Teacher, I've been thinking about what you said. Does this really mean this . . . ?'

When we looked at Jesus' miracles we saw how, for better or for worse, they divided people: challenging them into either accepting or rejecting him. The parables do the same. Sadly, for some people, Jesus' teaching did not have an educational impact at all: it simply confirmed that they had already rejected God.

JESUS' TEACHING: THE POWER AND THE PASSION

There was an astounding authority to Jesus' teaching. Most of the religious teaching of his day was based on tradition. If a teacher making a statement wanted to give it authority, he would always refer to the rabbis who had made it before: 'Rabbi Samuel following Rabbi Ezekiel following Rabbi Benjamin said . . .' Such statements had a stale and second-hand air about them. In contrast, when Jesus taught, he often began by saying 'you have heard it said, but I say to you'. The personal authority that Jesus claimed was something that people found striking. The result was that 'the crowds were amazed at his teaching, for he taught as one who had real authority – quite unlike the teachers of religious law.'[20]

But there was far more to Jesus the teacher than some cool, academic verbal brilliance; there was an intense passion to his teaching. What drove that passion was that he cared for his hearers. 'When he saw the crowds, he had compassion on them, because they were harassed and helpless, like sheep without a shepherd.'[21] Jesus' love was not just for the human race as some anonymous mass; he also cared for people as individual men and women.[22]

That Jesus had such a love for people explains why, at times, he expressed anger. Jesus was angry when he saw the religious leaders were objecting to him healing on the Sabbath,[23] when he saw the temple turned into a market place,[24] when children were prevented from coming to him[25] and when he met those who had turned religion from a blessing into a curse.[26] True love cares enough to get angry at injustice. The absence of anger that is often praised today may be a vice, not a virtue: what passes for tolerance may actually be apathy. There *is* such a thing as righteous anger. Jesus' anger was merely the other side of his love.

WHAT JESUS TAUGHT

The great theme of Jesus' teaching was that, with his appearance, something extraordinary had happened: God was acting in history in a new and unprecedented way. Jesus used many ways to talk about this new intervention of God. The commonest involved the idea of 'the Kingdom of God'. The gospels mention the Kingdom over eighty times and it is the subject of nearly two-thirds of Jesus' parables.* Jesus saw the coming of the Kingdom as the basis of the Good News – the Gospel.[1]

---

* In John's Gospel, God's actions in Jesus are seen not so much as the coming of the Kingdom, but more as the coming into the world of God's life, light and love. And in the Letters, the emphasis is much more on 'being saved', 'being made right with God' or 'knowing Jesus'. Yet the basic teaching of the New Testament is everywhere the same: God has entered the world in Jesus and begun a new era in which he can be known as 'Father'.

UNDERSTANDING THE KINGDOM

It is easiest to understand the Kingdom of God by seeing it as God's way of putting the world right, as his rescue programme for the human race. Because of our rebellion against God, we are separated from him. Our attempt to 'go it alone' has been a catastrophe: instead of gaining freedom, we have found ourselves enslaved to evil. Although God could have just crushed this rebellion by force, he didn't. Instead, he launched an alternative strategy, a long and costly process of trying to bring the human race back to himself. The Bible identifies three phases to this great labour of love: a phase of preparation and then two phases of the Kingdom. The phase of preparation is long over and the first phase of the Kingdom, begun by Jesus coming to our world, still continues today. The second phase of the Kingdom will begin with Jesus' return in what is called 'the Second Coming' and it will last for ever.

The 'Phase of Preparation' is what we read about in the Old Testament. In it, we see how God prepared the way for his kingdom. He chose a people, Israel, and taught them about himself and what his standards were. Towards the end of this long period of preparation, God made promises of a new kingdom that would be different and far greater than any of the earthly and limited kingdoms that Israel had so far known. One of a number of prophecies about the Kingdom in the book of Daniel says this: 'During the reigns of those kings, the

God of heaven will set up a kingdom that will never be destroyed; no one will ever conquer it. It will shatter all these kingdoms into nothingness, but it will stand for ever.'[2] This new kingdom would be one that would challenge and defeat all the other kingdoms and empires of the world.

For centuries after Daniel these other kings and kingdoms continued to crush God's people underfoot. Finally, John the Baptist came with the startling declaration that at last the Kingdom was 'at hand'.

History was about to enter a new phase.

Phase One: the present Kingdom of God

Jesus' announcement of the coming of the Kingdom was a declaration that the time of preparation was over. In his ministry of teaching, healing and deliverance from evil, the Kingdom was beginning. People could now enter the Kingdom and Jesus saw his Spirit-empowered actions as a visible proof that the Kingdom was present.[3] Much of Jesus' teaching applies to this phase of the Kingdom and therefore applies to us now.

As the parable of the mustard seed taught, the Kingdom is at present hidden and easy to overlook. This apparent insignificance of the Kingdom posed problems for some of Jesus' hearers; they expected something more dramatic. Jesus taught that the Kingdom's appearance as something weak and vulnerable is deceptive; it is, in fact, a powerful and active force for change in lives and situations. Like yeast in dough, it works slowly and silently.[4] In spite of its apparent insignificance, the Kingdom is unstoppable because it is God's work, and his authority and power are behind it.[5] Unlike the Old Testament kingdoms, the Kingdom of God knows neither geographic boundaries nor ethnic or racial restrictions; its extent is global and people from all nations will enter it.[6] In this present phase, the Kingdom is open for all to enter it.

Precisely because the Kingdom represents God's power at work, it is actively opposed by the devil's forces. This world is the scene of a fierce and persistent spiritual battle, largely unseen by us, between the Kingdom and its enemies.[7] As part of that battle, the coming of the Kingdom stirs up all sorts of things, both good and evil: not everything that claims to be part of the Kingdom is genuine and comes from God.[8] In this phase of the Kingdom, the authentic and the counterfeit coexist.

The New Testament makes it clear that the Kingdom of God is centred on Jesus. He preaches the Kingdom, brings it into being and leads it. He is still at the heart of the Kingdom. Today, as in the past, people only enter the Kingdom by finding the king, Jesus.

Phase Two: the future Kingdom of God

Jesus did not limit his teaching to this first period of the Kingdom. He also talked about a second phase, the final glorious coming of the Kingdom. Although Jesus only gave limited teaching on this future time, the general picture is clear.

This second phase will begin when Jesus returns from heaven: an event that will be sudden, unexpected and unmistakeable.[9] It will bring with it the judgement of good and evil and the final destruction of the Devil.[10] As a result, this eternal and glorious Kingdom will be totally free from all that is evil and wrong.[11] This phase of the Kingdom will be very different to the present[12] but the images Jesus gives indicate that it is a wonderful place where people from all over the world are gathered in peace and joy.[13]

Yet the coming of the Kingdom in this final state will also mark the end of the invitation to enter: with Jesus' return, the door that is open at present will be closed.[14]

The idea of the eternal Kingdom ought to affect how we live and ought also to transform our idea of death. For the follower of Jesus, death is not an end; it is instead a direct short cut to the excitement, joy and glory of the eternal Kingdom.

ENTERING THE KINGDOM

The importance of the Kingdom

The gospels make it clear that nothing is more important than belonging to the Kingdom: to enter it is to gain 'eternal life' and it is to 'be saved'.[15] In one of Jesus' parables, we read that the Kingdom 'is like a pearl merchant in search of choice pearls.

When he discovered a pearl of great value, he sold everything he owned and bought it!'[16] The Kingdom is so valuable that no expense or sacrifice is too great to enter it. Another of Jesus' sayings sums up the importance of the Kingdom: 'And how do you benefit if you gain the whole world but lose your own soul in the process?'[17]

If to be in this future Kingdom will be to know unspeakable joy, to miss it will be to suffer unspeakable loss. No language is adequate to express the sorrow of failing to enter the Kingdom.[18] To lose the Kingdom is to lose everything for ever.

How to enter the Kingdom

One of the most remarkable things about the Kingdom is that it is free. We cannot earn the Kingdom; we can only receive it as a gift.[19] Jesus says to his disciples: 'It gives your Father great happiness to give you the Kingdom.'[20] It is no wonder the announcement of the Kingdom is called 'the *Good* News'.

But to gain the Kingdom requires action. The parable of the pearl of great value does not just teach that the Kingdom is valuable; it teaches that you have to act to get into it. Jesus talked about the Kingdom as having a narrow gate that needs to be searched for.[21]

So how is the Kingdom entered? The basis of entry is to have an obedient trust in Jesus, the King. The gospels tell how, when some parents brought their little children to Jesus to be blessed, he used the infants to make a point: 'the Kingdom of

God belongs to such as these. I assure you, anyone who does not have their kind of faith will never get into the Kingdom of God.'[22] To have such a faith is to have a simple, personal trust in Jesus. Luke gives an example of this when he tells us how, when Jesus was hanging on the cross, one of the criminals being crucified next to him turned to him and said 'Jesus, remember me when you come into your Kingdom.' Jesus' reply was 'I assure you, today you will be with me in paradise.'[23] That simple trust alone was enough for Jesus to be able to promise him forgiveness.

Yet because being in the Kingdom is to be under the rule of the King, two other conditions exist.

The first is *repentance*, the complete rejection of and turning away from everything that is wrong and opposed to the Kingdom. Announcing the coming of the Kingdom, Jesus says 'Turn from your sins and believe this Good News!'[24] To repent is to choose to reject anything that will get in the way of the Kingdom. Bad actions and bad desires: all must be discarded. If the seeds of God's Kingdom are to grow in our lives, then all the old weeds need to be cleared away first.

The second is *commitment*. To enter the Kingdom also involves taking Jesus as king of our lives. It means being committed to him as Lord and being obedient to his rule. This may sound like giving up our freedom, but the gospels make it clear that outside the Kingdom, no one is free. Because we are all ruled by our own desires and the pressures placed upon us, to come into the Kingdom is to be liberated. Using an image from how animals were harnessed, Jesus said: 'Come to me, all of you who are weary and carry heavy burdens, and I will give you rest. Take my yoke upon you. Let me teach you, because I am humble and gentle, and you will find rest for your souls. For my yoke fits perfectly, and the burden I give you is light.'[25]

This commitment to follow Jesus into the Kingdom has to be sustained. Jesus warned that there would be those who, although they received the news of the Kingdom with joy, would fail to continue in it. Their commitment would be found to be merely one of words and inadequate to deal with life's pressures or temptations.[26] Life in the Kingdom is not a hundred-metre dash; it is more like a marathon.

So while the Kingdom is free, it makes demands. It is precisely because of these demands that Jesus cautioned those who were interested in the Kingdom to think things through seriously before following him. In any conflict of priorities, the Kingdom must come first.[27]

LIVING IN THE KINGDOM

Jesus saw entering the Kingdom as something so fundamental and life-changing that it is like being born again.[28] And, like being born, it is a beginning rather than an ending. Much of

Jesus' teaching on the Kingdom was on how to live as a citizen of the Kingdom.

Two errors have been made about Jesus' teaching on how to live the life of the Kingdom. The first is to imagine that trying to be good grants you entry into the Kingdom. That is wrong: the clear teaching of Jesus is that the Kingdom is a gift, not a reward. The second error is to think that entry into the Kingdom excludes the need to try to be good. It doesn't: Jesus expected his followers to live out lives that were good, pure and moral. Being good is neither an entry requirement to the Kingdom nor an optional extra for those who live in it.

Jesus saw living in the Kingdom as something that was drastically new.[29] The newness of the Kingdom shows itself in many areas.

A new relationship to God

Jesus said very little about God that was not already found in the Old Testament. He revealed only two new things about God, yet both were of earth-shaking significance.

Firstly, Jesus taught that God could be known as 'Father'. He addressed God as such in his prayers and he taught his disciples to use the same term in their own prayers. In fact, the Aramaic term he used, *Abba*,[30] which can be translated as 'Daddy', 'Dad' or 'Dear Father', was so characteristic of Jesus that twenty or more years later, even Greek-speaking Christians knew and used it.[31] Jesus' use of the term 'Father' for

God, with its overtones of closeness and confidence, was revolutionary. In the Jewish faith of his day, God could be known as 'Lord' or 'King' but he had become a distant figure who was rarely, if ever, addressed as 'Father'. Jesus taught that this ease of access to God as Father was not simply for him alone: it was the privilege of all his followers too. The prayer that Jesus gave his followers as a pattern to base their own praying on – the Lord's Prayer[32] – begins 'Our Father.' All those who have come to God through Jesus are God's children and can have a relationship of trust and confidence with God.*

Secondly, a key part of Jesus' teaching about God was the awesome claim that he, Jesus, was God. This is something so important that we will look carefully at it in the next chapter.

New standards

Jesus set new standards for his people. Rather than just repeat the Old Testament Law as it was understood in his day, he took it, cleaned away all the things that had been added to it and reapplied it. This is seen in a passage in Matthew's Gospel that has become known as the Sermon on the Mount.[33] The

---

* The idea of God being our Father shouldn't be seen as something that emphasises the 'maleness' of God. Neither does it say that 'God is like your Father'; something that, sadly, for many people might be very bad news. Its purpose is primarily to encourage us to have a close and confident relationship with God.

problem with the Law was that it was easy to treat it as something that only dealt with actions. So the sixth of the Ten Commandments stated: 'you shall not murder'. Most people looked at that and ticked it off as a commandment they had fulfilled: then, as now, few people committed actual murder. Yet Jesus took the commandment deeper than just actions, applying it also to the mind, and condemned anger as the root of murder.[34] He did the same with adultery and condemned lust as its root.[35] Religion had been based on actions, but Jesus brought motives and desires under God's judgement. He believed the people of the Kingdom were not simply to perform good acts; they were to *be* good.[36] As Jesus himself said, only good trees can produce good fruit.[37] With Jesus, religious purity was no longer about external actions; it was about internal attitudes.[38]

Jesus also broadened the Law. The Law had become limited to being good and kind to friends and relatives. Jesus taught this was inadequate: you had to love even your enemies.[39]

Jesus summarized the standards of the Kingdom like this: "'You must love the Lord your God with all your heart, all your soul, and all your mind." This is the first and greatest commandment. A second is equally important: "Love your neighbour as yourself." All the other commandments and all the demands of the prophets are based on these two commandments.'[40]

Jesus set a high standard for life. Critics have alleged that he set his standard so high that it is impossible. Such a view overlooks three things. The first is that Jesus and his followers considered the Kingdom 'good news', so they didn't see it as something that produced only failures. The second is that Jesus' followers know God as a loving heavenly Father who for-gives those who acknowledge with sorrow their failure to keep his standards and who encourages them to try again. The third is that God gives his people the gift of his Holy Spirit to help them live out life in the Kingdom. In John's Gospel we read how, in the middle of telling the disciples of the coming of the Holy Spirit, Jesus explained to them that they could only bear fruit (that is, live good lives) if they remained in him: 'for a branch cannot produce fruit if it is severed from the vine, and you cannot be fruitful apart from me.'[41] The purpose of the Holy Spirit is to be a helper who will allow us to be related in this 'fruitful' way to Jesus. Receiving the Spirit, obeying his guidance and knowing his empowering is what enables us to live the sort of lives that God wants.[42]

New lifestyle

The gospels record many of Jesus' instructions on how life in the Kingdom is to be lived. His teaching describes the follow-ing characteristics of those who are in the Kingdom:

- *Integrity*. The citizens of the Kingdom are those who are totally trustworthy. They do what they promise and do not need to make oaths or vows to strengthen their promises.[43]

- *Consistency*. Jesus' followers practise what they preach and do not concentrate on trivial matters at the expense of major ones.[44] The hypocrisy and distorted faith that characterized some of Jesus' contemporaries should be absent in the Kingdom.

- *Prayer*. Those who are in God's kingdom pray with faith and confidence for themselves, for others and for the coming of God's kingdom.[45] Their praying is not a matter of self-glorifying public performance or of empty words but is simple and sincere.[46]

- *Forgiveness*. Because God has freely forgiven those who are in the Kingdom, they forgive others.[47] There is no place for revenge in the Kingdom.[48]

- *Humility*. No one gets into the Kingdom on their own merits, so there are no grounds for boasting and no basis for pride or self-importance. For similar reasons, there should be no critical and loveless judging of others.[49]

- *Service*. There is to be no arrogance or sense of superiority among those who live in God's kingdom: instead, there should be the desire to serve one another. Jesus saw himself as a servant and expected his followers to imitate his example.[50]

- *A right attitude to wealth and possessions*. Jesus spoke a good deal about how we handle possessions and money. He pointed out that although both are good things, they pose dangers. They provide a misleading illusion of security and can all too easily become preoccupations that get in the way of loving God.[51] Those in the Kingdom are to hold lightly to both wealth and possessions and be prepared to give them away.

- *Love for one another*. The Kingdom is to be made up of people who care for one another. On the night of his betrayal, Jesus said this to his followers: 'So now I am giving you a new commandment: Love each other. Just as I have loved you, you should love each other. Your love for one another will prove to the world that you are my disciples.'[52]

- *Joy*. Those in the Kingdom should be joyful. After all, they are secure in the knowledge that God cares for them.[53]

- *Hope*. Those who are in the Kingdom can be confident in the future. The Kingdom that is already here and enjoyed is just a foretaste of that great and eternal Kingdom whose coming is certain. Mixed with that hope is also a longing. The Lord's Prayer has an important line in it: 'May your Kingdom come soon. May your will be done here on earth, just as it is in heaven.'[54]

At the beginning of the Sermon on the Mount, Jesus gave a memorable portrait of the character of those who belong to the Kingdom:

'God blesses those who realize their need for him, for the
Kingdom of Heaven is given to them.

God blesses those who mourn, for they will be comforted.

God blesses those who are gentle and lowly, for the whole
earth will belong to them.

God blesses those who are hungry and thirsty for justice, for
they will receive it in full.

God blesses those who are merciful, for they will be shown
mercy.

God blesses those whose hearts are pure, for they will see
God.

God blesses those who work for peace, for they will be called
the children of God.

God blesses those who are persecuted because they live for
God, for the Kingdom of Heaven is theirs.'[55]

The character that Jesus described as being appropriate to the
Kingdom surprised and astounded his hearers. It has not lost
its shock value.

WHO WAS JESUS?

J esus talked a great deal about the Kingdom, but he also spoke much about who he was. In considering Jesus' identity we are faced with two questions. Who did Jesus claim to be? And was that claim true?

Evidence for who Jesus thought he was can be seen in various areas: his views of his mission, the titles he used for himself, the actions he performed and the claims that he made.

JESUS' VIEW OF HIS MISSION

How Jesus saw himself is reflected in the way that he saw his mission; that can be summed up in four images:

Royal Rescuer

To a Jew, the high point of the Old Testament was when God, through Moses, rescued his people from slavery in Egypt. Jesus saw himself as doing something very similar: he too was some-one who had come to set people free. The words ' 'salvation', 'saviour', 'redeem' and 'redeemer' which occur throughout the gospels all express a series of ideas related to being rescued, whether physically or spiritually.[1]

Jesus' name is significant: Jesus ('Yeshua') means 'Yahweh saves'.[2] At Jesus' birth we are told that he is the promised Saviour and the one who will save his people from their sins.[3] Jesus defined his mission with the following words from the Old Testament:

'The Spirit of the Lord is upon me,

for he has appointed me to preach Good News to the poor.

He has sent me to proclaim

that captives will be released,

that the blind will see,

that the downtrodden will be freed from their oppressors,

and that the time of the Lord's favour has come.'[4]

Jesus saw himself as the great rescuer and deliverer of his people.

Loving Leader

If the image of a royal rescuer seems too military for us, it is balanced by another picture of Jesus as the one who lovingly leads and protects his people. Jesus came to a people who had lost their way and offered to lead them back to God. We read: 'When he saw the crowds, he had compassion on them, because they were harassed and helpless, like sheep without a shepherd.'[5]

Jesus saw himself as the great shepherd, the one who came to guide, recover and protect the lost. There is no contradiction between this caring leadership and that of the royal rescuer; after all, shepherds fight to defend their sheep. As leader, Jesus offered his gentle rule as a lighter load to those struggling with the unbearable burden of keeping the religious laws and traditions.[6]

Jesus claimed he had come to be a ruler who protected and guided his people.

Perfect Provider

Jesus also declared that he was the one who provided for all his people's needs. The feeding of the five thousand, the healing of the sick, the deliverance from demonic oppression, the raising of the dead: they are all examples of how Jesus provides perfectly in every situation.

The idea that Jesus is the one who completely provides for his people's needs is summed up by the seven great statements he makes about himself that are recorded in John's gospel:

- 'I am the bread of life. No one who comes to me will ever be hungry again.'
- 'I am the light of the world. If you follow me, you won't be stumbling through the darkness, because you will have the light that leads to life.'

- 'I am the gate for the sheep. . . . Those who come in through me will be saved.'
- 'I am the good shepherd. The good shepherd lays down his life for the sheep.'
- 'I am the resurrection and the life. Those who believe in me, even though they die like everyone else, will live again.'
- 'I am the way, the truth, and the life. No one can come to the Father except through me.'
- 'I am the vine; you are the branches. Those who remain in me, and I in them, will produce much fruit. For apart from me you can do nothing.'[7]

These seven statements show Jesus claiming to be the complete answer to our every requirement, both now and for ever. Whether there is a need for guidance, comfort, protection or an answer to issues of guilt and death, Jesus is the one who is able to help.

Suffering Servant

The fourth image of Jesus in the gospels is one that is particularly remarkable. Jesus talked about himself as being a servant and suffering in the place of those he served. So, after rebuking his followers for their pride and selfishness, Jesus said: 'For even I, the Son of Man, came here not to be served but to serve others, and to give my life as a ransom for many.'[8] Jesus claimed to be Lord and King; but he also declared that he was a lowly servant and, more amazing still, one who would willingly suffer for others.

Behind this saying of Jesus lies one of the most significant of all the Old Testament prophecies. In Isaiah there is a description of a Servant of the LORD, a mighty figure who would come and, despite his high rank, be rejected, suffer and die on behalf of others.[9]

The astonishing idea that Jesus saw himself as this Servant, who had come both to serve and to die for others, occurs in all the gospels. In John's Gospel, Jesus says: 'I am the good shepherd. The good shepherd lays down his life for the sheep.'[10] John the Baptist even referred to Jesus in terms of a sacrificial animal, calling him 'the Lamb of God who takes away the sin of the world'.[11]

Jesus claimed by his words and his actions that he was the Messiah, God's king, yet he chose to serve and suffer for his people.

HIS TITLES

The various titles either used by Jesus of himself or given to him are vital in understanding who he saw himself to be. Here are some of the main titles used:

Messiah

The first Christians were so certain that Jesus was God's promised king or Messiah that the names 'Jesus' and 'Christ' (from

Christos, the Greek translation of 'Messiah') became almost interchangeable. Jesus, however, rarely used the title 'Messiah' of himself, presumably because of its nationalistic and revolutionary overtones. When he did, it appears to have only been where it was practical for him to do so. So, for instance, Jesus declared to a Samaritan woman that he was the Messiah; but the Samaritans were hardly going to cause trouble in Jerusalem. And when Jesus did accept the title 'Messiah' from the disciples, he gave them a warning to keep it private.[12] Linked with 'Messiah' is the title of 'Son of David',[13] a reference to the promised king who would come from the line of David.

Son of God

Jesus directly referred to himself as 'the Son of God' and taught parables that implied that title for himself.[14] At Jesus' baptism and at the transfiguration, a voice from heaven confirmed that Jesus was God's son. In the gospels other figures, including demons, Satan and a Roman centurion, also call Jesus the 'Son of God'. These references link to the promises in the Old Testament that one day God would install a king who would be 'his son'.[15]

But what does 'Son of God' mean? In Jesus' culture, the closest human relationship was that between father and son. Strange as it may seem to us with our knowledge of genetics, it was felt that a son was effectively the continuation of his father; there was a direct and undiluted link between the two. What a father was, his son was.

So how was Jesus the Son of God?

First, *Jesus stands in the place of the Father*. Even today in many traditional Middle Eastern countries if you go to meet an important man and only meet his son, there is no reason to feel disappointed. The son can stand in the place of the father and be relied on to speak for him; any promises that he makes will be honoured by his father. Jesus represents this situation exactly: he is one with his Father and can say: 'Anyone who has seen me has seen the Father.'[16]

Second, *Jesus knows the Father perfectly*. Jesus has such an intimate personal fellowship with God that he can call him 'Abba, Dear Father'. So close is this relationship that Jesus knows exactly his Father's thoughts and wishes. He can say 'My Father has given me authority over everything. No one really knows the Son except the Father, and no one really knows the Father except the Son and those to whom the Son chooses to reveal him.'[17] Jesus could speak for his Father because he knew him.

Third, *Jesus is faithful to the Father's will*. As the perfect son, Jesus does exactly what the Father wants and shows perfect obedience and trust. At both Jesus' baptism and the transfiguration, God announces his pleasure at his son's obedience.[18]

Fourth, *the Father loves the Son*. The gospels clearly show there is a love between the Father and the Son that parallels that which exists between human parents and their children. It is precisely because of this intense love that the Father giving Jesus up to death is so moving. Jesus' death was not some cold and unfeeling transaction but an intense sacrifice by both Father and Son.

Although Jesus taught his followers that they could know God as Father, he made a distinction between his unique relationship to God and theirs. He speaks of 'my Father' and 'your Father'[19] and of himself as God's 'one and only Son'.[20]

Son of Man

The title 'Son of Man' was Jesus' preferred title for himself. At first glance, 'Son of Man' is a rather odd and insignificant phrase. It could be used as an indirect way of talking about yourself or, as 'a son of man', it could simply mean 'a man'. Certainly, to the Roman authorities, the term would have been utterly meaningless and totally unthreatening. Yet to Jews who knew their Scriptures, it was a very different matter. Jesus referred to himself not as 'a son of man' but 'the Son of Man'. In doing so, he was referring to one of the most significant passages about the Kingdom in the Old Testament. In the Book of Daniel there are several visions and in one of them Daniel sees God – 'the Ancient One' – sit on a throne and begin to judge the world.

As my vision continued that night, I saw someone who looked like a Son of Man coming with the clouds of heaven. He approached the Ancient One and was led into his presence. He was given authority, honour, and royal power over all the nations of the world, so that people of every race and nation and language would obey him. His rule is eternal – it will never end. His kingdom will never be destroyed.'[21]

This Son of Man is an awesome figure who is worthy of worship. He is also associated with the Kingdom of God coming with power: this universal and eternal kingdom is his. In some places, Jesus' use of the term 'the Son of Man' for himself is unmistakably linked with this passage, as when he is tried before the Sanhedrin: there Jesus' declaration that he is the Son of Man who will sit 'at God's right hand' provokes uproar and cries of blasphemy.[22]

By saying he was '*the* Son of Man' Jesus was claiming to be the king of the eternal Kingdom.

Lord

The Greek word translated as 'Lord' has several meanings in the gospels. Sometimes, when people call Jesus 'Lord' they are simply being respectful and the word means no more than 'Sir'. Yet the word 'Lord' was also used as a term for God and, in some cases, when it is used of Jesus it is a divine title. This is particularly true when Jesus refers to himself as '*the* Lord'.[23]

The first Christians were in no doubt that to call Jesus 'Lord' was to give him the very highest title. So, early in Acts, Peter concludes a speech with this claim: 'So let it be clearly known by everyone in Israel that God has made this Jesus whom you crucified to be both Lord and Messiah!'[24] In the early church, the most basic statement of belief was to call Jesus Christ 'Lord'.[25]

Other titles

Other titles are used in the gospels for Jesus. On one occasion, Jesus was referred to as 'God'. When the resurrected Jesus confronted Thomas the disciple, his response was to exclaim 'My Lord and my God!'[26]

More subtle, but no less powerful, claims are presented when Jesus makes the great 'I am' statements in John's Gospel: 'I am the bread of life', 'the light of the world', 'the living water', etc.[27] Jesus made the astonishing declaration that he *personally* was all these things.

One use of the little phrase 'I Am' goes even further. During a discussion with Jesus, his hostile opponents referred to their ancestor, Abraham. Jesus responded 'Truly, truly, before Abraham was, I Am.'[28] Here Jesus was not just claiming to have existed before Abraham (which would have been remarkable enough); he was using the phrase 'I AM', which was the name that God had used of himself when he spoke to Moses.[29]

HIS ACTIONS

How we act reflects how we see ourselves. A number of Jesus' actions reveal that he saw himself as much more than a good human being or even a prophet:

- Jesus summoned the twelve disciples in a way that indicated that he personally was going to recreate or restore the twelve tribes of Israel. As it was God who had made Israel, Jesus' claim to remake it is very striking.
- Jesus' entry into Jerusalem on Palm Sunday was a deliberate public claim to be the Messiah.
- At the Last Supper, Jesus talked with his disciples about a 'new covenant'.[30] However, as the covenant was the central bond in the relationship between God and his people Israel, Jesus' claim to be replacing that first covenant is breathtaking. It assumes he considered himself to be equal to the maker of the first covenant.

In addition to these actions, Jesus also performed miracles. As we noted in Chapter 9, the range and style of these extraordinary actions point to Jesus being divine.

HIS CLAIMS

In what he said, and how he said it, Jesus made direct and indirect claims about who he was:

- From the extraordinary authority that Jesus claimed it is apparent that he knew he was no ordinary teacher or prophet. For instance, at the end of the Sermon on the Mount Jesus said: 'Anyone who listens to my teaching and obeys me is wise, like a person who builds a house on solid rock.'[31] Someone who was only a prophet would have mentioned God here: Jesus mentions himself.

- Jesus frequently used the word 'Amen' or 'truly' to introduce his sayings. This is something that seems to have been unique to Jesus and a way of claiming absolute and ultimate truth for his words. It suggests that Jesus believed he was equal to God.

- Jesus claimed to be able to forgive sins.[32] Since every Jew knew that only God could forgive sins, to say this was to make a claim to be God.

- Jesus claimed the right to make definitive interpretations of the Law of God.[33] He reinterpreted the Law and redefined how it should be applied.[34] Jesus did not even justify his changes: he simply said 'But I say'.

- Jesus saw himself as greater than any figure of the Old Testament. He claimed to be greater than Jonah, Solomon, Jacob and even Abraham.[35] Jesus said that John the Baptist was the greatest man who had ever lived, but implied that he was greater.[36]

- Although the temple was considered to be the dwelling place of God, Jesus claimed that he was superior to it.[37]

Jesus even suggested that his own body was the temple.[38]

- The Sabbath day was one of the great distinguishing features of Judaism and considered to be the gift of God. Yet Jesus said: 'I, the Son of Man, am master even of the Sabbath.'[39]

- Jesus claimed that his words would outlast heaven and earth.[40]

- Jesus claimed that total authority on earth had been given to him.[41]

- Jesus claimed that how people responded to him would decide their eternal destiny.[42]

- Jesus stated that he would be the judge on the Day of Judgement.[43]

- Jesus claimed that he must take complete precedence over his follower's family, friends and career.[44]

- Jesus accepted worship, prayer and faith. He commanded people to pray in his name.[45] He invited people to put their faith in him and praised them when they did.[46]

- Jesus taught that what people did to him they did to God.[47]

It is also worth noting that in several places in the gospels Jesus implied that he was not limited by either time or space. When Jesus spoke about his past, he stated that he had come from heaven[48] and had existed before Abraham.[49] Talking of the future, Jesus said that he would return to heaven[50] and promised his disciples that he would be with them for ever.[51] The implication is that Jesus saw himself as eternal, something echoed by John's description of him as 'the Word'.[52] Equally extraordinary was Jesus' claim, when sending the disciples out to the 'ends of the earth', that he would be with them wherever they went.[53]

As only God is eternal and present everywhere, Jesus' claims are very striking.

WHO DID JESUS THINK HE WAS?

If we look at all the evidence, the conclusion is unavoidable that Jesus saw himself as being God. In a variety of ways, Jesus showed that he considered himself to be God; that he was God's Son; the Lord, the Son of Man, the 'I AM'. Certainly, as the letters of the New Testament show, the earliest Christians considered Jesus to be someone who was God and whom they could worship.[54]

In considering this claim, we need to remember that Jesus was speaking in the Jewish world, which fervently believed there was only one God. If Jesus had been an Eastern mystic or a New Age teacher, for him to say that he was God would not have been a big issue; in such belief systems we are all, in some way, divine. But in Judaism there was only one God.

! HOW COULD JESUS BE BOTH MAN AND GOD?

The traditional Christian view of Jesus is that he was both perfectly God and perfectly human. Yet this raises an important issue: how can God and man coexist in the same body? After all, while human beings have limited power and knowledge, God's power and knowledge are unlimited. So how, practically, did it work? For instance, did the young Jesus ever get the wrong answer at school? Did he ever face the frustration that we all face when trying to learn a language?

On the whole, the church has given two answers to such questions: the first is to ignore them and pass on swiftly and the second is to say we don't know and it is pointless speculating. Neither answer is satisfactory. In fact, many people assume that it is quite impossible that Jesus could be both truly God and truly human.

The first thing to say is that this is an undeniably complex area and there is a lot we do not understand. Nevertheless, some helpful suggestions have been made, and we repeat them here because they may help those who find such matters troubling.

The issue of God's power is easier to deal with than God's knowledge, so let's start there. The Bible presents Jesus as someone who was able to exercise divine power and authority, in that he could do such things as calm storms, raise the dead, heal the sick and turn water into wine. Yet it seems obvious that for Jesus to be truly human, he could not be an invulnerable and all-powerful being. Clark Kent may have been the 'Man of Steel' but we aren't, and Jesus wasn't either. And this is not simply something that we deduce from theoretical arguments; the fact is that the gospels portray Jesus as being totally and completely human: he was tired,[55] hungry,[56] thirsty[57] and ultimately he was killed. So presumably, although Jesus had access to God's power, there were times when he did not choose to use it. There is a hint of this when Jesus stops his disciples defending him at his arrest: 'Don't you realize that I could ask my Father for thousands of angels to protect us, and he would send them instantly?'[58] Presumably, Jesus only used such power as he knew his heavenly Father would want him to use.

Such a principle no doubt also applied to the issue of how much Jesus knew. Clearly, Jesus did know many things that ordinary people cannot know,[59] yet there were some things he was not aware of.[60] Luke's reference to Jesus growing 'both in height and in wisdom'[61] implies that Jesus learnt as we do. It seems that while Jesus always had a right to divine knowledge and could have used it, he only made use of such knowledge as he knew his heavenly Father wanted him to. Jesus allowed his obedience to his Father to limit both his power and his knowledge.

Such a suggestion not only helps us make sense of how someone who was God could at the same time be totally human, it also shows us a Jesus who is a helpful model of obedience. The book of Genesis tells how the human race's slip into rebellion began with disobedience against God. The gospels tell us that the answer to this rebellion came when Jesus lived out an entire life of obedience to God.

The New Testament does not try to answer how Jesus is God and how he relates to the Father; it simply 'tells it like it is'. For the gospel writers, the mechanics of how the incarnation worked are not the issue. Ultimately, all we really need to know is that in Jesus, God came to this world to reach out to us.

CONSIDERING THE CLAIMS OF JESUS

Jesus' claims are so awesome and significant that they cannot simply be ignored or overlooked. If Jesus was, in some way, God come to earth, and if our eternal happiness does depend on us giving him our total loyalty, then we are faced with an issue that is without any doubt the most important thing in the world.

Equally, if the claims of Jesus to be God's unique and supreme intervention into our world are to be rejected with any intellectual honesty, then some alternative explanation for them must be found. Yet the alternatives are very limited. One assessment of Jesus sixty years ago by C.S. Lewis was that because of Jesus' claims, there were only two alternatives to him being Lord: he was either a liar or a lunatic. With the passage of time, we might extend and rephrase those alternatives: Jesus was either mythical, misunderstood, mistaken, mentally disturbed or someone who misled his followers.

Was Jesus *mythical?*

This first alternative is an attempt to duck the challenge. This 'escape route' from the claims of Jesus assumes the gospels are unreliable and that the divine figure they portray is fictional. Yet the gospels show none of the hallmarks of myth; they are understated and matter-of-fact accounts and the evidence that Jesus considered himself much more than a man is so diverse (the direct and indirect claims, the titles, the actions) and, above all, so consistent, that it seems far more probable that the figure they portray is authentic.

To maintain such a view a hard question has to be answered: *how did such a mythical Jesus arise?* How did a belief that 'Jesus was a good man' so rapidly evolve into 'Jesus was God'? There are no remotely similar parallels for this sort of development elsewhere, and none at all in Judaism.

Was Jesus *misunderstood?*

This second alternative suggests that, in reality, Jesus never claimed to be God. Rather, his disciples spectacularly misinterpreted what he said and turned his claim to be a faithful prophet of God into that of being an incarnation of God. This view might have some merit if Jesus' claim to be divine rested on one single statement; but given that he presented his claims in so many different ways it seems hard to maintain. It is difficult to believe that Jesus' disciples were so stunningly in competent that they consistently and repeat-edly misunderstood what he said on one of the most fundamental issues of his teaching. The charge of ineptitude can also be extended to the leaders of the early church, for never thinking to check whether the disciples had got it all wrong.

Was Jesus *mistaken?*

A third alternative is that it was Jesus himself who was wrong. On this view, Jesus genuinely thought he was God but, in reality, was sadly mistaken about his own identity. This would mean, however, that far from Jesus being a reliable and authoritative interpreter of the Law, he was breaking the First Commandment – 'you shall have no other gods before me' – in a most breathtaking and blasphemous way. The implications of this view are devastating: if Jesus was wrong about this most fundamental issue, then nothing else that he said can be trusted. If he was wrong here, Jesus was not even a reliable teacher.

Was Jesus *mentally disturbed?*

Another alternative is that Jesus suffered from a delusional psychological disorder. So, for example, the writer George Bernard Shaw considered that Jesus must have suffered from megalomania. Such an explanation has one slight merit: it admits Jesus did make astonishing claims about himself. Yet there is little else to support it. In the gospels, Jesus does not come over as the slightest bit delusional or disturbed.

To hold this view requires you to believe that the greatest moral influence the world has ever seen was a man who was mentally disturbed. That conclusion is so bizarre and unsettling that few people have felt comfortable even considering it.

Did Jesus *mislead* his followers?

A final alternative is that in making his claims, Jesus deliberately misled his followers: he lied to them. Yet it is hard to imagine any motive for Jesus wanting to mislead people in this way; far from leading to fame or fortune, his claims merely led to his death. And the charge of lying hardly seems consistent with everything else that we know of Jesus, including the fact that he started many of his statements by saying '*Truly*, I say to you...' To pretend to be God and to accept the worship and praise of devout followers, while you knew you were as human as they were, would be an extraordinary act of deception. To say that it seems out of character with the author of the Sermon on the Mount is an understatement!

CONCLUSIONS

Jesus made extraordinary claims that he was God. If those claims are true then they have awesome and life-changing implications. In Jesus, every search for God comes to its end. In him is found everything that our hearts truly desire and that our lives really need.

There are alternative explanations for the claims that Jesus made. Yet none of those explanations is without serious flaws. A Christian could easily say that it takes much less faith to believe that Jesus made his claims to be God because that's who he was, than to believe the alternatives. One of Sherlock Holmes' comments to Watson is helpful here: 'It is an old maxim of mine that when you have excluded the impossible, whatever remains, however improbable, must be the truth.'

One event that we will look at later and that is crucial to Jesus' claims is the Resurrection. If Jesus did rise from the dead, then all his claims are confirmed as true.

Finally, simply saying 'I believe Jesus is God' does not exhaust the significance of Jesus' identity. It is too easy to limit the idea that Jesus is the divine Son of God to some theoretical test-question that identifies true Christianity. Yet to be a Christian does not mean to obey a doctrine or recite a creed, it is to live within a transforming relationship with Jesus. The reality is that the idea that Jesus is God is a truth that should sustain us every day. Jesus was not just the Royal Rescuer, Loving Leader, Perfect Provider and Suffering Servant for his people two thousand years ago: he is all those things for us *today*.

THE LAST WEEK

One of the most intriguing features of the gospels is the way that they focus on Jesus' death. So, in John's Gospel, chapters 1–12 cover three years, while chapters 13–21 cover just the single week of the crucifixion. This focus on the cross highlights the conviction of the gospel writers that Jesus' death was the reason for which he came.

PALM SUNDAY

All four gospels[1] describe Jesus' entry into Jerusalem on what the church calls 'Palm Sunday'. Although this event is often called the 'Triumphal Entry', any note of triumph is muted. That Jesus was going to enter Jerusalem was apparently known and expected; while in the past Jesus had hidden his actions and avoided confrontation, that time had now ended.

At Passover, Jerusalem overflowed with pilgrims; crowds followed Jesus and met him at the entrance to the city. They were excited and expectant: Passover was a feast that celebrated a past liberation by God from foreign oppression and looked forward to a new liberation in the future by the Messiah. At Passover, messianic hopes ran high and this year those hopes found a focus in Jesus.

The crowds welcomed Jesus enthusiastically by throwing their cloaks and palm branches before him and crying out: 'Praise God! Bless the one who comes in the name of the Lord! Bless the coming kingdom of our ancestor David! Praise God in highest heaven!'[2] John tells us that they also shouted 'Hail to the King of Israel!'[3]

These verses from the Scriptures, the references to 'the coming kingdom' and, above all, to 'the King of Israel' reveal the people's hope that Jesus would be the Messiah. The palm branches too were significant: two centuries earlier, when the victorious Judas Maccabeus had entered Jerusalem after liberating it from the Greeks, palm branches had been used during the processions.[4]

But Jesus – as ever – followed his own script. He rode in on a young and previously unridden donkey. It was a deliberate reference to an important prophecy about the Messiah in Zechariah: 'Rejoice greatly, O people of Zion! Shout in triumph, O people of Jerusalem! Look, your king is coming to you. He is righteous and victorious, yet he is humble, riding on a donkey – even on a donkey's colt.'[5] By entering this way, Jesus was making an unmistakable claim to be the Messiah. Yet he was at the same time deliberately rejecting the role of the military or political Messiah that people expected: the white horses, the banners, the swords and the soldiers of the conquering king were absent. The rumours of the arrival of a possible Messiah might have alarmed the Roman authorities; but Jesus' appearance on a young donkey, in weakness and gentleness, would have reduced any sense of threat.

No doubt many in the crowd expected that Jesus would do something spectacular when he entered Jerusalem. They were disappointed: instead of confronting the Romans, Jesus simply went to the temple, looked around carefully and then returned to Bethany, where he and his followers were staying. By the end of that Sunday, there may already have been those in Jerusalem who were feeling disappointed and disillusioned with Jesus.

MONDAY TO WEDNESDAY

After lodging in Bethany, Jesus re-entered Jerusalem on the following day. On the way, he saw a fig tree that already had a full show of leaves, normally a sign that small edible fig shoots could be found on it.[6] Yet despite the promise of fruit, the tree bore none and Jesus pronounced judgement on it: 'May no one ever eat your fruit again!' Later, it was seen to have withered. The link that both Matthew and Mark make between this – the only miracle of destruction in the gospels – and the clearing of the temple shows that it is an acted parable. Despite promising much, the nation and the temple system had produced no fruit. Judgement loomed. As the fig tree had withered at Jesus' word, so would the nation.

Jesus then went to the temple and drove the merchants and their customers from the outer court of the Gentiles.[7] The key to Jesus' action lies in the verses he quoted: 'The Scriptures declare, "My temple will be called a place of prayer for all nations," but you have turned it into a den of thieves.' The first part of the quotation refers to a passage in Isaiah which talks of God's wish to bless the Gentiles, the second to a passage in Jeremiah where the prophet announces judgement on the temple of his day because of the people's corruption.[8] Jesus was both rebuking the sense of national complacency that existed and also sounding a note of doom. His action was not that of God's reformer hoping for change, it was of God's prophet announcing that it was too late to change. Yet Jesus' statement looked beyond the temple's destruction in AD 70 to something else. Very shortly, Jesus, acting as temple, priest and sacrifice, would replace the temple and through him the whole world would be able to come to God.

On the Tuesday, Jesus returned to Jerusalem for a full day of teaching.[9] The day was marked by confrontation. Jesus appeared again in the temple where he was soon involved in controversy. A delegation from the Sanhedrin turned up[10] and questioned Jesus about the source of his authority. Jesus' answer was that it came from the same place as that of John the Baptist. As the religious leaders did not dare to admit – or deny – that John's authority was from God, they were forced into a humiliating silence.

Jesus also told some parables in which he confronted the religious leadership. Some of them spoke of impending judgement on the religious establishment, others unmistakably taught that he saw himself as God's Son.[11] Jesus also challenged his hearers about the identity of the Messiah. In these encounters, Jesus is increasingly open about his identity and the leaders are increasingly hostile to him.

On this day, Jesus also taught about both the near and distant future.[12] As they were leaving the temple, the disciples drew Jesus' attention to its magnificence. Jesus' response was startling: 'Do you see all these buildings? I assure you, they will be so completely demolished that not one stone will be left on top of another!'[13] Later, sitting on the Mount of Olives looking across at the great edifice of the temple, the disciples, still perturbed by Jesus' words, asked him 'When will this happen, and what will be the sign of your coming and of the end of the age?'[14] Clearly, they assumed the temple's destruction and Jesus' return would occur together. In his answer, Jesus separates these two events. Referring to the destruction of the temple, Jesus said there would be warning signs and warned his followers to flee the scene. Referring to his own return, Jesus implied that it would not be immediate: there would be a long and turbulent period when the good news about him would be proclaimed in the face of bitter opposition. There would be rumours of his return and false Messiahs would appear, but his followers should ignore them: when he did return it would be an event that was unexpected, unmistakable and unavoidable. As for the time of his return, Jesus said that it was something that only the Father knew.[15] The key issue for his followers was, he stressed, to be faithful and to be ready at all times for his return.

While we do not know what Jesus did on the Wednesday, we can be almost certain the religious leaders met then to consider their options.[16] Tuesday's confrontations in the temple had confirmed that Jesus had to be dealt with. He was undermining their authority, making blasphemous claims and, worst of all, threatening the delicate balance of power which gave the Romans security and taxes while allowing them prestige and prosperity. Jesus' claim to be the Messiah, his popular support and his sheer unpredictability threatened to cause a catastrophe. Friday evening would see the start of the Passover feast, and with it the heightened expectation of God's intervention. Jesus was too dangerous to be allowed to remain at large; they had to act fast and have him dead by sunset on Friday.

Achieving that objective posed problems. The Sanhedrin had no powers to put people to death, so any execution had to be a Roman one. However, having Jesus crucified by the Romans would have one great, if brutal, advantage. The Scriptures stated that anyone who was 'hung on a tree' was cursed[17] and there could be no surer way of destroying Jesus' claims to be the Messiah than by having him publicly shamed and cursed by God.

But how to arrest Jesus? He retained great support among the volatile crowd. A high-profile confrontation in daylight in the narrow and crowded streets of Jerusalem could trigger civil disturbances which would, in turn, incur Roman reprisals. An alternative and more discreet way of arresting Jesus had to be found. Here, conveniently, Judas Iscariot entered the equation.[18] By agreeing to betray Jesus, Judas made things easier. With inside knowledge, the leadership could now be tipped off as to where Jesus could be safely arrested.

Why Judas betrayed Jesus has been the subject of endless discussion. Unless it was a down payment, the money offered him – the infamous 'thirty pieces of silver' – was not a great amount. It is far more probable that Judas had become disillusioned. It may be that, perhaps alone of the Twelve, Judas had seen that Jesus had chosen to be a suffering servant rather than a ruling king and he didn't want to be part of it. Ultimately, though, his motives elude us.

THE LAST SUPPER

Towards the evening of the Thursday, Jesus and his followers gathered for a meal, the 'Last Supper', in a large upper room in Jerusalem.[19] The arrangements were made in secret, presumably to prevent Jesus' arrest. Time was running out for the religious leaders and they must have been getting desperate. Yet there is no hint of urgency or desperation in Jesus' attitude or actions at the meal: he remains in total control of events.

From Luke's Gospel we learn that despite having spent so long with Jesus, the disciples were still squabbling with one another over rank and status.[20] John tells us that before the meal began, Jesus addressed this issue in an extraordinarily dramatic way. He took a towel and, despite the protests of the disciples, washed the dust and dirt off their feet.[21] By performing a task so humble that it was done only by the lowest of servants, Jesus demonstrated that the only model for leadership was that of the servant.

The Passover meal was traditionally a family meal, and that evening Jesus presided over it in the manner of the head of the household. Traditionally, too, symbolic actions and ritual questions would be used to bring out the meaning of the Passover as a commemoration of God's deliverance. During this Passover meal, however, Jesus departed from the normal question and answer. Suddenly, his followers found they were no longer commemorating the Old Covenant; they were now celebrating something different, a New Covenant.

Taking the bread, Jesus broke it, saying 'This is my body, which is given for you.' Then, taking the cup of wine, he said: 'This is my blood, which seals the new covenant between God and his people. It is poured out to forgive the sins of many.'

Jesus' words included several references to the Scriptures. In establishing the first covenant, Moses had sprinkled the blood from sacrificed animals over the people, saying 'This blood confirms the covenant the LORD has made with you in giving you these laws.'[22] The first covenant had also involved a meal: immediately after Moses had sprinkled the blood, he and the leaders of Israel had gone up Mount Sinai and 'shared a meal together in God's presence.'[23] By echoing those words, Jesus was indicating the new covenant that he brought would also be put into effect with blood, but that the blood involved would be far more precious. The idea of a 'new covenant' was also a familiar one: God had promised long ago through Jeremiah that one day there would be a new covenant 'for the forgiveness of sin'.[24]

Through the unforgettable images of bread to be eaten and wine to be drunk, Jesus was teaching that his torn flesh and his shed blood were to be given 'for you'. He was indicating that his impending death was not going to be an accident or a meaningless tragedy, but something deliberately done for his followers. Jesus saw himself going to stand in the place of his followers and to bear the judgement that was theirs. His death was going to achieve something: it was to be a sacrifice, a ransom, and the payment of a penalty that would allow the forgiveness of sins.

By telling his followers that they were to 'do this in remembrance' of him,[25] Jesus was also saying that this meal was not a one-off action. As the Passover was a yearly reminder of the first great deliverance by God and the giving of the first covenant, so the sharing of the bread and the wine was to be repeated regularly to act as a reminder of God's greater deliverance in Jesus and the new covenant. Under various names – the Communion, the Breaking of Bread, the Eucharist, the Lord's Supper, the Mass – Christians have re-enacted this taking of bread and wine ever since. It is a reminder of two facts: that forgiveness is given to those who receive Jesus and that such forgiveness was bought for us at an astonishing cost.

After this, Jesus talked again about his betrayal and told John that he knew it was Judas who would betray him.[26] With Jesus' permission, Judas left, taking to the priests the knowledge they needed: Jesus would be spending the night in Gethsemane, an isolated walled garden, where he could be arrested.

Immediately after Judas' departure, Jesus predicted that all the disciples would desert him. Peter, however, was boastfully confident: the others might desert Jesus but *he* would follow him even to death. Jesus replied that before the cock crowed, Peter would have denied him, not just once but three times.

In John's Gospel, we are given an account of what Jesus said to his disciples following Judas' departure.[27] He told them that he needed to 'go away' but that this was not a disaster that should trouble them; his departure would be for their benefit. Jesus promised to return and also to send them 'another helper', the Holy Spirit who would guide and empower them and do for them what he himself had so far done. Jesus warned his followers that they had a mission which would not be easy; the world would be hostile towards them. He also instructed them to show love to one another. Yet the final note was one of encouragement: they could rejoice – in Jesus they had overcome the world.

Jesus followed his teaching with an extraordinary prayer which gives an unsurpassed glimpse into his relationship with his Father.[28] We see in this prayer the unity and love that exists between Father and Son, and Jesus' desire to complete the task he has been given. Finally, Jesus prayed for all who follow him – present and future – and particularly that they would be united in a way that would show who he is to the world.

Jesus and the disciples then left for Gethsemane.[29]

GETHSEMANE

What happened in Gethsemane is something both extraordinarily revealing and profoundly moving. Jesus called Peter, James and John to go with him as he went to pray. Then, leaving the three a short way behind him with instructions to stay alert, Jesus became overwhelmed with emotion. The descriptions leave nothing to the imagination: Jesus is described as 'throwing himself on the ground' and being filled with 'anguish' and 'deep distress'; in Luke we read that he was 'in such agony of spirit that his sweat fell to the ground like great drops of blood.'[30] These are remarkable descriptions: Jesus, who has been so far the master of every situation, is now assailed by the most agonizing emotions.

The focus of Jesus' intense anguish was what lay ahead: 'He prayed that, if it were possible, the awful hour awaiting him might pass him by. "Abba, Father," he said, "everything is possible for you. Please take this cup of suffering away from me. Yet I want your will, not mine."'[31] In the darkness of the garden, Jesus faced a final and almost overwhelming temptation to reject what lay ahead. He saw what the cross would cost him and was given a foretaste of the physical, mental and spiritual agony that he would suffer. The reason for the extraordinary depths of Jesus' distress here was, no doubt, not the awareness of the physical suffering of the crucifixion but the knowledge that on the cross he, the Son of God, would know for the first time utter separation from God the Father. Paul, writing to the Galatians, gives us an indication of what Jesus must have seen facing him: 'When he was hung on the cross, he took upon himself the curse for our wrong-doing. For it is written in the Scriptures, "Cursed is everyone who is hung on a tree."'[32]

The temptation for Jesus literally to walk away from the trial and the cross must have been powerful. Yet he resisted it and his praying ended with 'I want your will, not mine'. Jesus refused to rebel against his Father's will.

Twice, Jesus went to see if the three disciples were keeping watch with him but on both occasions he found them asleep.*
Jesus had never failed them but now, when he needed them, they failed him. Finally, he returned a third time to awaken the sleeping three. But now it was too late for further recriminations or apologies: the arrest party had arrived.

---

* Some people argue that because the three fell asleep, any record of what Jesus said must be imaginary. In fact, the disciples could easily have heard the beginning of what Jesus said, or he could have told them in the forty days of teaching after the resurrection. And anyway there were other people around in Gethsemane that night, including a mysterious young man (Mark 14:50–52) who may have been Mark himself.

THE TRIAL AND THE CROSS

O n the Friday of the Last Week, Jesus was arrested, tried and put to death in what has become the best-known trial and execution in history. The events of that day, from the arrest of Jesus to his burial, are recorded in detail by all four gospels. Their accounts do not make pleasant reading: the events were dominated by hatred, envy, mockery, cowardice, injustice and extreme brutality. The dreadfulness of the day is highlighted by the fact that the victim was totally innocent. In terms of the quantity of evil done, there have been many more terrible days in the history of the world, but in terms of the *quality* of evil, there has been none worse. For a day that has become known as 'Good Friday' (probably after the Old English word 'good', which meant 'holy') there seems precious little *good* about it.

THE ARREST

A large, armed crowd sent from the religious leadership and led by Judas arrived with a detachment of Roman soldiers in

Gethsemane in the early hours of Friday morning to arrest Jesus.[1] The temple leadership had, no doubt, found the cooperation of the Romans easy to obtain: the mention that a dangerous Messianic pretender was on the loose in Jerusalem at Passover would have guaranteed their fullest support. The use of overwhelming force to arrest Jesus was intended to crush any opposition and to prevent him from slipping away in the darkness.

Aware of the danger of misidentification in a darkness lit only by flickering torches and perhaps the Passover moon, Judas identified Jesus with a customary kiss of greeting. It was the first of many mocking and cruel acts that were to be inflicted on Jesus that day and it may have hurt him as much as any of them. The gospels tell us that Judas' act was pointless: Jesus readily declared who he was and asked that his followers be spared. There was a faint eruption of resistance as Peter lashed out with a sword and then, rebuked by Jesus, he and the other disciples fled.

Jesus, now on his own, was arrested, bound and taken away.

THE TRIALS OF JESUS

Each of the gospel writers reports that, following his arrest, Jesus underwent various legal examinations and procedures.[2] Although there is some uncertainty about the details, it is clear there were two separate sets of trials. In the first, Jesus was tried by the Jewish religious court of the Sanhedrin and found guilty of the religious offence of blasphemy, for which the penalty was death. However, since the Sanhedrin did not have the power to inflict the death sentence, they then handed Jesus over to the Romans for a second trial. Here Pontius Pilate, the Roman governor, examined Jesus on the political charges of rebellion and declaring himself to be a king, an offence of high treason punishable by crucifixion.

THE JEWISH TRIAL

The preliminary hearing before Annas

From John's Gospel we learn that Jesus was first taken to the home of Annas, the man who had been the high priest from AD 6 to 15. Although the Romans appointed men to this post and removed them as they saw fit, the high priest had traditionally been appointed for life and some people evidently still considered that Annas was the 'proper' high priest. He retained a vast influence and the current high priest, Caiaphas, was his son-in-law.[3] On the verge of a problematic trial, the leadership needed to make sure that Annas and his influence were behind them. This informal first hearing may also have been intended to probe what defence Jesus would offer. Annas asked Jesus about his followers and what his teaching had been. Jesus' response that it was public knowledge earned him a blow to the face: the first of many physical attacks.

The trial before Caiaphas

Shortly afterwards, while it was still night, Jesus was brought before Caiaphas, the man who was officially the high priest.[4] With him were enough of the Sanhedrin to make any verdict valid. Witnesses were summoned against Jesus, apparently with the intention of showing that he had threatened the temple, but they could not agree on their statements and Jesus remained silent. Finally, the high priest resorted to putting Jesus under solemn oath: 'I demand in the name of the living God that you tell us whether you are the Messiah, the Son of God.'[5] No faithful Jew could ignore such a charge and Jesus answered 'Yes, it is as you say. And in the future you will see me, the Son of Man, sitting at God's right hand in the place of power and coming back on the clouds of heaven.'[6]

His statement produced uproar: 'The high priest tore his clothing to show his outrage, shouting "Blasphemy! Why do we need other witnesses? You have all heard his blasphemy."'[7] By applying Daniel's prophecy to himself,[8] Jesus was not just acknowledging that he was the Messiah, he was claiming to be equal to God. The verdict was inevitable: Jesus was guilty and should die.

Dawn was breaking as Jesus, mocked and struck yet again, was led away. The first phase of his trial was over; he had been convicted of blasphemy.

Peter and Judas

The gospel writers weave the fate of two of the Twelve into their accounts of Jesus' trial before the Sanhedrin. Peter, his natural bravado returning and, no doubt, feeling bound by his oath of faithfulness, had followed Jesus into the courtyard of Annas' house.[9] There, as he stood around in the darkness, Peter found bystanders and servants asking him questions. Wasn't he a Galilean? Hadn't he been with Jesus? Hadn't he been in Gethsemane? Peter denied each question with increasing force, finally swearing with an oath that he didn't know Jesus. After his third denial, the cock crowed: Peter remembered Jesus' prophecy and broke down in tears. Far from following Jesus to death as he had promised, Peter had disowned him at the merest hint of danger.

The gospels also briefly mention the fate of Judas. On hearing that Jesus had been condemned to death, Judas was struck with grief and guilt. He returned to an unsympathetic temple leadership, threw away the money he had been paid and then, in utter despair, went and hanged himself.

THE ROMAN TRIAL

Jesus was now brought before Pontius Pilate, the governor, and the one man who could approve a death sentence. The other historical reports of Pilate that we have paint him as a man who was insensitive and brutal and who probably disliked

Jews. Nevertheless, it is worth remembering he served as governor of Judea for eleven years and must have had some merits as an administrator.

The Sanhedrin presented Jesus to Pilate as someone who by claiming to be 'the King of the Jews' had committed the capital offence of high treason. They were presumably hoping that Pilate would just rubber-stamp their request for an execution. But things were not that simple: Pilate turned out to be reluctant to agree to their demands. He must have already known something about Jesus from his soldiers' involvement in the arrest in Gethsemane and he probably already had suspicions that he was being dragged in to settle an internal Jewish dispute. Yet, as his questioning of Jesus persisted, Pilate became increasingly convinced the man before him was innocent. Finally, he announced to the priests and the crowd that had gathered outside the palace that he saw no basis for the allegations.

The angry response of the crowd – that Jesus had stirred up trouble all the way from Galilee – showed Pilate that they would be content with nothing less than the death sentence, but it also suggested a way out. Herod Antipas was in town for the Passover and, as ruler of Galilee, had the authority to pass judgement on Jesus. Trying to dodge responsibility, Pilate sent Jesus to Herod. He may have hoped that Antipas would take Jesus back with him to Galilee and, as he had done with John the Baptist, remove him from circulation. Luke's brief account of Jesus' interrogation before Antipas suggests that one of history's more dysfunctional dynasties hadn't changed for the better.[10] While the religious leaders shouted accusations, Herod treated Jesus as a conjuror, throwing question after question at him in the hope of seeing a miracle. Jesus stayed silent and Herod's frustration turned to mockery. Yet Herod did no more than mock. Dressing Jesus in 'a royal robe' – perhaps one of his cast-offs – he had him returned to Pilate.

Pilate, reluctant either to sentence Jesus or to risk the crowd's anger by freeing him, tried a new ploy. He offered to release a prisoner as a Passover gesture of goodwill, his hope being that the crowd would choose Jesus. Here too he was thwarted: the crowds, prompted by the priests, demanded instead the release of Barabbas, a criminal guilty of murder and rebellion.[11]

Increasingly frustrated and not wanting to be seen to yield to Jewish pressure, Pilate now tried yet another approach. He had Jesus flogged, presumably hoping that this would be enough to appease Jesus' enemies. Almost certainly what Jesus suffered was the most severe form of Roman flogging, using cords with metal-tipped lashes which ripped open the skin, tore into muscles and even exposed internal organs.[12] It was a punishment so severe that it sometimes caused death. Then, amid more blows and mocking, Pilate's soldiers placed a crown of thorns on Jesus' head and put a purple robe on him. Pilate now presented this battered and bleeding figure to the crowd.

Any hope that this brutal humiliation might satisfy them was dashed when the priests and temple guards began shouting 'Crucify! Crucify!'[13]

Pilate, by now exasperated at the turn of events, declared that he found Jesus not guilty. The leaders' response that Jesus 'ought to die because he called himself the Son of God'[14] merely stiffened Pilate's reluctance by frightening him: like most Romans, Pilate was probably intensely superstitious. He made yet another attempt to have Jesus released. This time the leadership played their last card, telling the governor 'If you release this man, you are not a friend of Caesar. Anyone who declares himself a king is a rebel against Caesar.'[15] It was a worrying threat that if Pilate released Jesus they would send a delegation to Rome to tell the Emperor Tiberius that he was disloyal. For Pilate, this was the deciding factor. He made one more feeble appeal to the crowd for Jesus to be acquitted ('Shall I crucify your king?')[16] but, frustrated yet again, yielded to their demands. He pronounced a formal sentence of death and washed his hands publicly as a gesture that he personally was not guilty. Jesus was sent for execution.

By condemning Jesus to a brutal death, despite being convinced of his innocence, Pilate was guilty of a terrible crime. Yet the outcome of Jesus' trial before Rome's representative was not simply the result of one man's personal weaknesses. Whether Pilate understood it or not, there was a real conflict between what Rome stood for and what Jesus did. Jesus' values were humility, love, service and forgiveness and they were in total opposition to Rome's values of might, majesty, authority and ruthless power. Ultimately, Jesus *was* an enemy of Rome.

! WHO WAS TO BLAME?

Some sceptical authors consider that much of the biblical account of Jesus' trial is invented and that, to win favour with their Roman rulers, the early church rewrote history to throw the blame onto the Jews and exonerate the Romans. Such a view implies the gospel accounts are an early form of anti-Semitism. As evidence, such authors point out that Jesus' trial before the Sanhedrin breaks many of the rules for the conduct of trials in the Jewish legal code, the *Mishnah*. Several responses can be made:

- The Mishnah was only written down around AD 200. Not only was this a long time after these events, but by then Judaism was very different to what it had been around AD 30. In Jesus' day, Sadducees, a group which ceased to exist in AD 70, ran the Sanhedrin. We simply do not know enough about the pre-AD 70 Jewish legal system to say how illegal this trial was.

- The Romans are hardly exonerated; every gospel makes it clear that it was they who authorized the brutal execution of an innocent man. Pilate, in particular, comes over very badly as Rome's representative. He is portrayed as a man who knew the charges against Jesus were bogus but who agreed, out of fear, to have him executed.

- The blame for Jesus' death is attributed by Josephus, himself a Jew, to the Jewish leaders.[17]

- The Sanhedrin wanted Jesus executed, but not just because they had some sadistic hatred of a harmless rural preacher; a major motive in their actions was that they were afraid Jesus could trigger precisely the sort of appalling Roman action that did occur forty years later.[18] Like many people since, they felt that in the case of 'a threat to national security', legal safeguards could be put to one side.

- The idea that the Bible makes an entire race of people guilty for Jesus' death is unfounded. If the New Testament places the blame on any one group, it is specifically on the Jewish leadership of the day. In fact, some of the earliest Christian preaching blames everybody: 'For Herod Antipas, Pontius Pilate the governor, the Gentiles, and the people of Israel were all united against Jesus.'[19]

- A far wiser approach to the issue of the blame for Jesus' death is to see our own condemnation in what happened. In doing what they did, the leaders were only doing what comes naturally to us all. If we look hard enough at our motives, we can see in ourselves the same fear, cynicism and selfishness that motivated the

Sanhedrin. It is a brave person who can say 'If I had been there, I would not have agreed to that verdict.'

THE CRUCIFIXION

When it comes to describing Jesus' death by crucifixion, the gospel writers make no attempt to arouse our emotions: they simply state what happened.[20] Yet what happened was horrific.

For the Romans, the point about crucifixion was not that it was an appropriate punishment for criminals but that it deterred crime. The Roman writer Quintilian said: 'Whenever we crucify the guilty, the most crowded roads are chosen, where most people can see and be moved by this fear. For penalties relate not so much to retribution as to their exemplary effect.'[21] The value of crucifixion lay in the fact that it was a horrible way to die.

Although there were variations in the details of crucifixion, the basic principle was the same. The man – almost all victims were men – had his arms fixed by ropes or large nails hammered through the wrists* to a crossbeam that was then raised and slotted into a vertical post. The feet were then nailed to the upright and the victim then simply left to die. With his weight supported

---

* The artists' image of Jesus being nailed to the cross through the palms of his hands is incorrect: the soft tissue there is not strong enough for such a purpose. The word translated in the Bible as 'hand' included the wrist.

largely by his legs, the victim found breathing agonizing, with every breath forcing him to push down on his nailed feet. For all the cruelty involved in fixing the victim to the cross, the process caused no major wounds to vital organs and death often occurred slowly. A crucified man could survive for days, suffering dehydration and sunstroke and, increasingly, becoming food for birds, animals and insects. Eventually, though, exhaustion would set in, the victim would become unable to lift up his head far enough from his chest to breathe, and death by suffocation would occur.

It was characteristic of Roman efficiency that they had developed a technology of crucifixion and could hasten or extend the duration of the suffering. Giving the victim a peg or a ridge to sit on delayed death, and breaking the leg bones – which made breathing harder – hastened it. The deterrent effect of crucifixion was enhanced by the way that it exposed the victim to public humiliation: stripped naked, unable to move, he could be mocked by all. Crucifixion was the most unheroic and appalling of deaths.

Under Roman guard, Jesus was taken to the place of execution. As was customary for convicted criminals, he was made to carry the crossbeam himself.* Weakened by the floggings, Jesus stumbled under the weight and the Romans ordered a

---

* The idea that Jesus carried the whole cross is another product of artistic imagination. The Romans found it more practical to keep the vertical beam permanently in the ground where it stood as a constant warning against rebellion.

passer-by, Simon of Cyrene, to carry the wooden beam.[22] The site of the crucifixion, at Golgotha ('the place of the skull'*), would have been somewhere prominent just outside the town walls where the maximum number of people could see what happened. There, in the late morning, Jesus was nailed to the cross.

The gospels provide some details about the crucifixion. Jesus was crucified between two other criminals. The grim procedure was supervised by a few Roman soldiers under the command of an officer, who passed the time gambling for Jesus' clothes. At the greatest moment in history, people were playing games. Of Jesus' followers, almost all had now deserted him. Only the women and one disciple, John, remained. The crowd gathered, including the curious and some of the religious leaders. It is an horrific but authentic insight into human nature that the mocking that had been directed at Jesus continued as he was pinned helpless to the cross.[23] Soldiers, bystanders, the religious leaders, even the criminals nailed next to him: all ridiculed him.

Above the cross, Pilate had arranged for a title to be fixed: 'Jesus of Nazareth, the King of the Jews.' It was written in three languages: Hebrew, Greek and Latin. As Pilate doubtless intended, the title infuriated the religious leadership. Pilate's

---

* Older English Bibles translated 'the place of the skull' with the word 'Calvary'.

petty attempt to retaliate for being outmanoeuvred allowed Jesus to die with his identity proclaimed above him.

The gospel writers see many of these details as the fulfilment of prophecy and their accounts are interwoven with references to the Scriptures, particularly Psalms 22 and 69. There seems little doubt that they also saw what happened that day as a remarkable fulfilment of Isaiah's prophecies of the Suffering Servant:

'Many were amazed when they saw him – beaten and bloodied, so disfigured one would scarcely know he was a person.'[24]

'He was despised and rejected – a man of sorrows, acquainted with bitterest grief. We turned our backs on him and looked the other way when he went by. He was despised, and we did not care.' [25]

'Yet it was our weaknesses he carried; it was our sorrows that weighed him down. And we thought his troubles were a punishment from God for his own sins! But he was wounded and crushed for our sins. He was beaten that we might have peace. He was whipped, and we were healed!'[26]

'He was oppressed and treated harshly, yet he never said a word. He was led as a lamb to the slaughter. And as a sheep is silent before the shearers, he did not open his mouth. From prison and trial they led him away to his death. But who

among the people realized that he was dying for their sins –
that he was suffering their punishment?'[27]

'He was counted among those who were sinners. He bore the
sins of many and interceded for sinners.'[28]

The early Christians were certain that, for all its dreadfulness,
what happened on the cross was no accident: it was the awesome culmination of God's age-old plan.

SEVEN SAYINGS FROM THE CROSS

The four gospel writers record seven sayings of Jesus from
the cross: what the church came to call the 'Seven Last
Words'. In these statements, uttered under such pain that
every syllable must have hurt, we see something of the meaning of the cross.

'Father, forgive these people, because they don't know what they are doing.' (Luke 23:34)

Jesus' first words from the cross were a prayer for forgiveness for
his persecutors. The hardest teaching Jesus ever gave was to 'love
your enemies'. Here, as ever, Jesus practised what he preached and
he showed exactly what he meant. By doing this, he established a
tradition of forgiveness that has continued through Stephen, the
first Christian martyr (Acts 7:60), to the present day.

'I assure you, today you will be with me in paradise.' (Luke 23:43)

Although both of the criminals hanging either side of Jesus began by mocking him, one changed his mind. He rebuked the other, declared that Jesus was innocent and asked Jesus to remember him 'when he came into his kingdom'. Jesus' response was: 'I assure you, today you will be with me in paradise.'

Jesus' answer is a powerful statement of his own authority. Even here, dying on the cross, Jesus still saw himself as having the power to save. In what he says there is not even a hint of a 'maybe' or 'I'll try to put in a good word for you', there is only a majestic certainty: 'Today you *will* be with me in Paradise.' Jesus' answer is also a tremendous expression of God's grace: it is an act of free forgiveness to someone who deserves nothing and who can do nothing to save himself. This incident has always been seen as an encouraging demonstration that last-minute conversions are possible and that there is a way back to God from the very edge of Hell.*

'Woman, here is your son.' 'Here is your mother.' (John 19:26–27)

Turning to his mother and to John, 'the disciple he loved', Jesus said to her, 'Woman, here is your son' and to him, 'Here is your mother.'

---

* That last-minute conversions are possible doesn't justify postponing any decision to follow Jesus. After all, who of us knows when our last minute will be?

John tells us that 'from then on this disciple took her into his home'.[29] Assuming that Joseph had died, Jesus, as the eldest son, would have been responsible for his mother and, with his other brothers still hostile to him, he now passed that responsibility on to John. Honouring parents was one of the Ten Commandments and Jesus' action here is a reminder that throughout his life he perfectly obeyed God's Law. It also shows us that even in appalling pain, Jesus cared for those who were dependent on him.

'My God, my God, why have you forsaken me?'(Mark 15:34)

Mark tells us that at noon, darkness descended on the land and as it fell, Jesus cried out in his native Aramaic 'My God, my God, why have you forsaken me?'

The darkness and Jesus' anguished cry are linked. We do not know what the cause of the darkness was. It was not an eclipse of the sun: eclipses cannot occur during Passover when there is a full moon, and it lasted for three hours. It might have been caused by a dense dust storm, a phenomenon known in the region at this time of year and one which can turn day into twilight. But whatever its origin, the gospel writers see the darkness as symbolic of what was happening. In the Bible, darkness is a symbol of judgement,[30] and now judgement was falling on the land and also on Jesus.

Jesus' cry, a quotation from Psalm 22:1, is the only recorded instance when Jesus does not pray to God as *Abba*, Father. The desperate prayer shows that although Jesus still trusted in God, he sensed that he was now separated from him and felt abandoned by him. For the first time in eternity, the unique fellowship between God the Father and God the Son was broken.

The gospel writers do not attempt to explain the meaning of Jesus' experience of abandonment and separation, but in the letters of the New Testament we find pointers to its meaning. So Paul says 'For God made Christ, who never sinned, to be the offering for our sin, so that we could be made right with God through Christ.'[31] At the very hour when the Passover lambs were being slain in the temple, Jesus, 'the Lamb of God who takes away the sin of the world',[32] was dying on the cross as a greater and ultimate sacrifice for sin.

'I am thirsty.' (John 19:28)

Jesus' statement of his thirst is a reminder of the bodily pain that was the physical counterpart of his spiritual agony. Again, there is a thought-provoking irony: he who had supplied all needs now suffers the most basic of human desires and the one who had offered 'living water' to the thirsty is now thirsty himself.

'It is finished.' (John 19:30)

John tells us that after Jesus had tasted the sour wine given to him by the soldiers, he said 'It is finished!' In the original Greek, 'it is finished' is a single word which, in this context, means 'it is fulfilled' or 'it is completed', and which was often stamped on paid bills. Jesus was not saying 'I am finished' but something different: that he had completed all he had come to do.[33] He had paid the price and offered the needed sacrifice.

'Father, I entrust my spirit into your hands!' (Luke 23:46)

The very last words of Jesus as he died were a simple childlike prayer committing himself to his Father. The spiritual darkness was over, he had surfaced from the terrible depths and he could now call God 'Father' again.

John's Gospel tells us how the Jewish leaders, not wanting to have the crucified men still hanging there on the Sabbath, asked Pilate for the deaths to be hastened. The soldiers duly broke the legs of the criminals either side of Jesus, but found that he was already dead. To make sure, one soldier stabbed Jesus in the side with a spear and 'blood and water flowed out'.[34] The precise medical explanation of this is debated, but it was clear evidence to the soldiers – who knew more about the practicalities of crucifixion than we do – that Jesus was dead. Jesus seems to have died unusually quickly for someone who was crucified. This may have been because he had already been flogged heavily and subjected to a considerable amount of other physical abuse earlier. Ultimately, though, Jesus is portrayed as laying down his life; even while submitting himself to death, he retained his control over it.

The gospel writers tell us of other incidents that occurred as Jesus was crucified. In addition to the darkness, there were two other events. The first was an earthquake, something not uncommon in the region. The second and more obvious event was that, as Jesus died, the curtain in the temple was torn from top to bottom.[35] Curtains were a key part of the temple and symbolized the separation that existed between sinful human beings and the holy God. The miraculous tearing of this curtain indicates two truths: men and women can now come to God directly through Jesus and the temple is now redundant.

The synoptic gospels also inform us that the Roman centurion who was supervising the execution declared Jesus innocent and said that he was 'truly the Son of God'.[36] In this confession of someone from beyond Israel that Jesus was God's Messiah we see the first indication of the vast number of Gentiles who would soon be coming to faith in Jesus.

In the darkness, an old age was ending and a new one beginning.

THE BURIAL

Normally, the corpse of someone who was crucified was thrown into a common grave, but if there was a request from the family, the body might be released to them. With Jesus, such an intervention came not from the family but from Joseph of Arimathea, a man who while being a member of the Sanhedrin had not agreed with its verdict.[37] Joseph went to Pilate and, courageously identifying with Jesus, asked the governor for the body. After ascertaining that Jesus was indeed dead, Pilate allowed Jesus' body to be taken down and handed over to Joseph.

With the Sabbath due to start around six that evening, Joseph did not have much time. Aided by Nicodemus, another member of the Sanhedrin who had been sympathetic to Jesus, he had Jesus' body taken down from the cross. It was taken to a tomb that Joseph had had cut into the rock nearby for his own eventual use, as was the custom. There Joseph and Nicodemus wrapped the body in a shroud, packed a large quantity of spices around it and placed it in the tomb. Finally, they had the large round stone rolled back across the entrance of the cave. The first three gospels mention a significant detail: the women who had followed him from Galilee watched Jesus' burial at a distance.

Night fell.

On the following day, the Sabbath, only one event is recorded. A delegation from the Sanhedrin visited Pilate and asked for the tomb to be guarded in order to 'prevent his disciples from coming and stealing his body and then telling everyone he came back to life'.[38] Pilate gave orders that the tomb be sealed and authorized a guard to be placed at it.[39] The tomb was duly sealed and guarded. The religious and political powers in the land had collaborated to see Jesus dead and buried; they now collaborated once more to ensure that he stayed that way.

THE GREAT EXCHANGE

The cross is the place where everything becomes overturned.

Innocence becomes guilt

The gospel writers detail the trials of Jesus not to show the guilt of the judges but to show the innocence of the defendant. All that Jesus had done wrong was to declare the truth: that he was the Son of God, the Messiah. No other charge was made against him. Yet in being crucified, Jesus was judged a criminal and executed between criminals.

Power becomes weakness

In the gospels, Jesus is a man of extraordinary power and authority; all things – wind and waves, food and drink, sickness and death – obey him. Jesus is the king of nature. Yet on the cross, Jesus lays all this aside: he becomes mocked and helpless, unable to move even his own hands and feet. 'Go on, save yourself,' jeer the leaders. 'You saved others, save yourself.'[40]

Fellowship becomes separation

All through his life Jesus had perfect fellowship with God, yet on the cross he becomes separated from him. Jesus knows God intimately as Father and rejoices in the access that he has to God, but on the cross a barrier descends between them.

Life becomes death

Jesus was the one who raised people from the dead, the one who declared that he was Life. Yet now he submits to death of the very worst kind. He of whom John could say 'Life itself was in him'[41] dies.

The key to understanding the cross is to be found in the words of Jesus at the Last Supper when he declared that the bread was his body broken 'for you' and the wine was his blood shed 'for you'. It is that repeated phrase *'for you'* that ultimately explains both the cross and Jesus. What happened at the cross was substitution.

The cross is the place of exchange. It is where Jesus descended to the depths so that we might ascend to the heights. It is where Jesus, out of love, became everything that we human beings are – guilty, weak, separated from God and subject to death – in order that we may, if we choose, share in his innocence, his power, his fellowship with God, his life.

And when you understand that, referring to the worst day in the history of the world as 'Good' Friday makes sense.

THE RESURRECTION

By all the precedents of history, by all the known laws of nature, the story of Jesus should have ended with his burial. Not only was Jesus dead, but he had been brutally and publicly killed in such a humiliating manner that it seemed clear to all that he was not – and never had been – God's Messiah. His followers had been humiliated and scattered. It was – very definitely – the end of the story.

But it wasn't. Something happened, something that transformed Jesus' followers and ultimately transformed the world, something that made the events of that Passover not the end of a story but the beginning of one. That this *something* was the resurrection of Jesus from the dead is the foundation of Christian belief, past and present.

Christianity would not exist without the resurrection. Around AD 53, Paul wrote to Christians in Corinth: 'If Christ was not raised, then all our preaching is useless, and your trust in God is useless . . . And if Christ has not been raised, then your faith is useless, and you are still under condemnation for your sins."[1] Paul was making the bold statement that the Christian faith stands or falls on the resurrection of Jesus.

The importance of the resurrection is still overwhelming. If the resurrection of Jesus *did* happen, then the implications are breathtaking. Everything the Bible says about Jesus is true: God can be known as Father, forgiveness is possible, heaven is attainable and death is just a short sleep before eternal joy. And if the resurrection of Jesus *didn't* happen, then the implications are equally breathtaking, but in the worst and most devastating way: the Bible cannot be trusted, God – if any such being exists – is a distant deity, there is no certainty of forgiveness, no assured hope, no confidence in the face of death. Whether or not the resurrection happened isn't just a fact of history; it is a fact that changes our future.

So as we look at the issues surrounding the resurrection we need to remember that, as it always did, everything hinges on whether it is true.

THE ACCOUNTS

Detailed information about the resurrection comes from six places in the Bible: the four gospels, Acts and a summary that Paul gives in 1 Corinthians 15:

'I passed on to you what was most important and what had also been passed on to me – that Christ died for our sins, just as the Scriptures said. He was buried, and he was raised from the dead on the third day, as the Scriptures said. He was seen by Peter and then by the twelve apostles. After that, he was seen by more than five hundred of his followers at one time, most of whom are still alive, though some have died by now. Then he was seen by James and later by all the apostles. Last of all, I saw him, too, long after the others, as though I had been born at the wrong time.'[2]

Paul's list is particularly significant as it is agreed that 1 Corinthians was written about twenty years after the crucifixion. It may therefore be the oldest statement of the resurrection that we have. Paul's reference to it having 'been passed on to me' suggests that the list is even older; it may even be what Paul was told when, after his conversion, he met the other apostles in Jerusalem around AD 35.[3]

The Christian belief that Jesus was raised from the dead centres on three lines of evidence: the empty tomb, the appearances themselves and the very existence of the Christian church.

THE EMPTY TOMB

All the gospels report that on the Sunday morning, Jesus' tomb was found to be empty and the body gone.[4] Although there are uncertainties about how the various accounts fit together, what seems to have happened is something like this.*

At dawn on the Sunday morning, the women returned to the tomb with spices. Although they had observed the burial of Jesus by Joseph of Arimathea and Nicodemus on the Friday afternoon, they now wanted to pay their own last respects to him and, no doubt, to make certain that the burial rituals had been properly carried out. Arriving at the tomb, they found the guards had fled and the large gravestone had been rolled away. Concluding that the tomb had been robbed, Mary Magdalene ran back to tell Peter and John. The other women peered into the empty tomb and were greeted by two angels, one of whom made the extraordinary statement that Jesus was not there: he had been raised just as he had promised. With feelings of joy, amazement and fear, the women ran away from the tomb. Alerted by Mary, Peter and John ran to the tomb and found it empty apart from the linen grave clothes and the cloth that had covered Jesus' head which was 'folded up and lying to the side'.[5] The two then left: Peter amazed, John beginning to believe that Jesus had risen.

To understand the significance of the empty tomb, we have to realise that the only sort of resurrection the Jews conceived

---

* One good attempt at harmonising where and when things happened is to be found in John Wenham's book *Easter Enigma: Are the Resurrection Accounts in Conflict?* (Paternoster, 1984).

of was one that involved the body. The mere appearance of someone after their death would have been considered a vision or the manifestation of a ghost or spirit, not a resurrection. So the fact that the tomb was empty fits with the biblical accounts that the appearances of Jesus after his death were a genuine resurrection involving the presence of a transformed physical body.

On its own, the empty tomb doesn't prove the resurrection took place; after all, there could be other reasons for a missing body. But it is good indirect evidence. Given the Jewish beliefs about the nature of a resurrection, it is impossible that any belief that Jesus had been resurrected could have spread had the body still been there in the tomb. Joseph was a wealthy and well-known man; his tomb was probably in a private garden that he owned and its location was, no doubt, public knowledge. All the Sanhedrin had to do was to have a public exhumation and all the tales of a resurrection would have collapsed. But they didn't do that and the reason was very simple: they couldn't. The body wasn't there.

THE APPEARANCES

The accounts of the empty tomb form merely the background to the central feature of the resurrection of Jesus: the reports that he appeared to numerous people over a period of forty days.

The four gospels, Acts and 1 Corinthians 15 mention around a dozen appearances of the resurrected Jesus:

The appearance to Mary Magdalene (John 20:11–18)

According to John, the very first resurrection appearance was to Mary Magdalene. After telling Peter and John the body had gone, Mary returned to the tomb. There she encountered Jesus, mistaking him for the gardener until he addressed her by name. Jesus told Mary to go and tell the others.

The appearance to the women (Matthew 28:8–10)

Jesus also appeared to the rest of the women as they left the garden. He told them not to fear and confirmed the message the angel at the tomb had given to them.

The appearance to Peter (Luke 24:34; 1 Corinthians 15:5)

There are two references to a private encounter, some time on the first Easter Sunday, between the risen Jesus and Peter, the man who had so badly failed him.

The appearance on the Emmaus road (Luke 24:13–34)

Luke tells how, in the late afternoon of Easter Sunday, two of Jesus' followers, Cleopas and an unnamed companion, were walking away from Jerusalem and talking about what had happened when they were joined by a man. In response to the stranger's enquiry, they told him what had happened to Jesus, mentioning – with evident mystification – the rumours they had heard of his resurrection. The stranger rebuked their disbelief and then began to explain the Scriptures to show the Messiah must suffer before 'entering his time of glory'. Arriving at their destination, Cleopas insisted that their friend join them for a meal; when the stranger broke bread, prayed over it and handed it to them, they suddenly realized it was Jesus. He disappeared and immediately the two started back towards Jerusalem to tell the other disciples.

The appearance to the disciples (Luke 24:35–43; John 20:19–23)

The disciples, still afraid of the religious leaders, met behind locked doors on the evening of Easter Sunday. Cleopas and his companion arrived and, as they were telling their story, Jesus appeared to all of them. Their immediate reaction was to be terrified that they were seeing a ghost. Jesus reassured them of his identity, encouraged them to touch him and then, as a final proof that he was not a ghost, asked for some food, which he ate.[6] Again, Jesus explained that what had happened to him had been predicted in the Scriptures and he promised the coming of the Holy Spirit.

The appearance to all the Eleven
(John 20:26–29)

Thomas, who had been absent from the Easter Sunday evening encounter, expressed scepticism about the accounts of a resurrection. Eight days later, as he and the disciples were again meeting behind closed doors, Jesus came and stood among them. Thomas, invited by Jesus to touch him, now believed, declaring 'My Lord and my God!'

The appearance by the Sea of Galilee
(John 21:1–23)

After this the disciples returned to Galilee and seven of them decided to go fishing overnight. Early in the morning, Jesus met them and ate breakfast with them. It was at this meeting that Peter was finally fully restored to fellowship.

The appearance to the disciples in Galilee
(Matthew 28:16–20)

Matthew ends his gospel with Jesus meeting his disciples in Galilee and giving them their instructions. There he told them: 'I have been given complete authority in heaven and on earth. Therefore, go and make disciples of all the nations, baptizing them in the name of the Father and the Son and the Holy Spirit. Teach these new disciples to obey all the commands I have given you. And be sure of this: I am with you always, even to the end of the age.'[7]

The appearance to more than five hundred followers (1 Corinthians 15:6)

In his list of resurrection appearances in 1 Corinthians, Paul records an appearance to 'more than five hundred of his followers at one time, most of whom are still alive'. Where and when this appearance took place is unknown.

The appearance to James (1 Corinthians 15:7)

Paul also says that Jesus appeared to James, his brother. Although we know nothing more about this appearance, it helps explain why James, who had previously not believed in Jesus, became a leader in the early church.[8]

Another appearance at a meal (Acts 1:3–5)

Close to the end of the forty-day period of appearances, Jesus showed himself to the disciples in Jerusalem again. At a meal with them, he told them to stay in Jerusalem until they were baptized with the Holy Spirit.

The Ascension (Luke 24:50–53; Acts 1:6–11)

Luke tells how, at the end of forty days, Jesus went a short way out of Jerusalem with the disciples to the Mount of Olives, where he ascended into heaven. This event, which the church calls the Ascension, was a visible illustration of two truths. The first is that the time of the resurrection appearances was now over; Jesus' earthly ministry was completed. The second is that from this point in history, Jesus is enthroned as king and rules in majesty in heaven.*

THE NATURE OF THE APPEARANCES

Several features of these appearances of the resurrected Jesus are notable:

- The appearances are varied. They occurred outdoors and indoors, to one, two or 'more than five hundred' people, at different times of day and in different places.
- The appearances are not visions but physical events. The Jesus who appears can be touched and felt. He prepares and eats food.
- The appearances are dynamic, rather than static. The Jesus who appears walks with people, does things and talks.
- The appearances of Jesus are lasting, rather than momentary. His followers didn't just get a fleeting glimpse of him; there was time for meals and conversation.
- The appearances are rather undramatic and unsensational. There are no fanfares of trumpets or flashes of

---

* The idea that Jesus is the king ruling in heaven is developed much further in the letters of the New Testament.

lightning: the risen Jesus just appears and then talks or eats with his followers.

- The appearances are unpredicted and unexpected.
- The Jesus who appears is, in some ways, just like the 'old' Jesus. Physically, he still bears the scars of the crucifixion. And after their initial shock, the disciples relate to him with the same intimacy and familiarity that they did before the crucifixion.
- In other ways, however, the Jesus who appears is different to what he was. He is able to appear and disappear at will: locked doors pose no barrier to him. Sometimes he isn't immediately recognized as being Jesus.

In summary, these appearances were of a real, physical, but somehow transformed Jesus. Paul sheds some light on matters when he suggests the risen Jesus is the first example of the glorious transformed bodies that Jesus' followers will one day have.[9] If we attempt to *explain* these appearances we find ourselves in difficulties. They are utterly unique and cannot be explained by science. But to try to deal with the resurrection with scientific explanations is to miss the point.

THE FACT OF THE EARLY CHURCH

For someone searching for the truth about the resurrection, these first two lines of evidence that we have been discussing are problematic: the appearances ended forty days after they had begun and the empty tomb is no longer available for examination. Yet there is a third piece of evidence, the existence of the church, and that is one that has convinced many people that the resurrection did occur.

If we think about the situation on the evening of Good Friday, it is clear that Jesus' followers had been totally shattered by what had happened. Against all expectations, Jesus had been crucified: an event that carried with it the implication that God himself had delivered a negative verdict on his claims. The catastrophe was deepened by the uncomfortable facts that Jesus had been betrayed from within the Twelve and that Peter, their leader, had himself denied Jesus. It was an utterly hopeless situation.

Yet seven weeks later, everything was astonishingly different. Peter and the other disciples were back in Jerusalem, openly and confidently declaring that the Jesus who had been crucified was the Messiah. Something had transformed the dispirited, disillusioned and discredited followers of Jesus into a dynamic, confident and expanding movement. The disciples claimed that what had transformed them was the appearance of the risen Jesus to them and his sending of his Spirit on them: no one has ever suggested a more plausible alternative.

Even those who take a highly sceptical view of the historical value of the gospels and Acts are faced with a problem. The history of the church is matter of hard and inescapable facts.

Within twenty years of the crucifixion, there were groups of people across the eastern Mediterranean worshipping the crucified Jesus as Lord and Messiah. Within a hundred years, large numbers of Christian communities had become established, often in the face of persecution, across most of the known world. The explosive growth of Christianity from the most discouraging start imaginable – a crucified Jewish manual worker and a handful of ordinary people – requires an explanation. The only satisfactory solution is that this extraordinary expansion was created by a combination of three extraordinary things: the person of Jesus, the phenomenon of the resurrection and the power of the Holy Spirit.

! THE RESURRECTION: SUPPORTING EVIDENCE

For many people, this is evidence enough that the resurrection did occur. Yet there are other pieces of evidence:

The nature of the resurrection accounts

The accounts in the gospels of the appearance of the risen Jesus to his followers do not resemble imaginary accounts or mythical events:

● Some of the gospel accounts have the definite air of being eyewitness reports. So, for instance, in John's account of the visit to the tomb[10] we have the statement that John 'outran Peter and got there first. He stooped and looked in and saw the linen cloth lying there, but he didn't go in.' These are the sort of incidental details that occur only in genuine eyewitness accounts or in realistic fiction. And no one had yet invented realistic fiction.

● There has been no attempt to harmonize the accounts to fit one particular official version of events. So Luke mentions that there were five women at the tomb; Mark, that there were three; Matthew, two and John, only one. There is no necessary contradiction here, but if the resurrection was an invented story, it's surprising that someone didn't tidy up the reports.

● There are a number of unexplained elements in the accounts. Why do the two on the Emmaus road not recognize Jesus at first? Why was Mary Magdalene told by Jesus 'Don't cling to me, for I haven't yet ascended to the Father'?[11] These are not major issues but you would expect invented accounts to be smoother.

● The disciples are portrayed in an unflattering light. Jesus rebukes them for their unbelief, their fear and their doubt.[12]

The location and time of the first claims of the resurrection
If the belief of the resurrection had sprung up years later and miles away from the time and place of the crucifixion

and burial, then we might suspect that we were dealing with a myth. Yet it didn't: the first preaching of the resurrection occurred within a few weeks of the events of the first Easter, within a mile or so of the place where Jesus had been buried and in front of people who had witnessed everything.[13]

The role of women as witnesses

In our culture we are inclined to overlook the extraordinary fact that the first witnesses to the resurrection were women. In Jewish culture at the time, women were not allowed to be legal witnesses. In the Talmud, the compilation of Jewish law, it is stated that: 'Though the woman is subject to the commandments, she is disqualified from giving evidence.'[14] It is significant that when, in 1 Corinthians 15, Paul recounts the appearances of Jesus, he specifically omits the appearances to women. He knew that his readers would not be convinced by evidence based on women's testimony. Had the resurrection accounts been invented, or even heavily rewritten, they would not have made so much of the testimony of women.

The unexpected nature of the resurrection

It seems clear that the resurrection was totally unexpected by the disciples. As faithful Jews they expected a resurrection at the end of time but not before then. The idea of a resurrected, crucified Messiah was a novelty to them. Indeed, the accounts suggest the risen Jesus had to explain to the disciples that his resurrection was both logical and predicted by the Scriptures. The disciples would hardly have manufactured the evidence for something that they didn't expect.

The early church's attitude to the resurrection

However deep people dig into the history of the Christian church, no level has ever been uncovered in which the resurrection of Jesus was not a central feature. In early Christian preaching there is no hint of any apology or unease about the resurrection, nor any suggestion that it was an invented explanation for the embarrassing fact of the crucifixion. Every sermon recorded in the book of Acts focuses on it. Throughout Acts and the Letters, there is an unshakeable and universal confidence that the resurrection of Jesus had really happened.

The changed Sabbath

The keeping of the Sabbath on Saturday was not an optional extra in Judaism: it was one of God's commandments and one of the distinctive features of the Jewish faith. Yet within a few years of the crucifixion, Jesus' followers, who had been devout Jews, had shifted the focus of their week to Sunday. It is hard to imagine anything capable of causing such a shift other than the resurrection.

The language used about Jesus

The earliest Christians considered Jesus was the Messiah, referred to him as 'Lord', prayed to him as God and assumed that he was with them. It is hard to believe that such beliefs could have developed if anybody knew that Jesus was really a rotting corpse in a Judean tomb.

The testimony of Paul

Paul's strong and early teaching on the reality of the resurrection is particularly striking given that no more than three or four years after the crucifixion, Paul was a leader of the religious establishment's task force in Jerusalem to persecute Christians.[15] In that position, he would have worked with the priests who had been involved in the Easter events and who would have known the 'official' explanation of the resurrection. Yet whatever that explanation was, Paul came to believe that Jesus had been raised.

The logic of the resurrection

The resurrection of Jesus may have been unexpected but it has its own logic. It is like one of those twists in a novel or film that takes you by surprise until you think about it, and then you realize that it actually makes sense and it fits with the plot. So the Old Testament teaches that death is the inevitable consequence of human beings having sinned against God. The interesting implication of this (which no one appears to have explored before the resurrection) is that if someone who had never sinned actually did die, death would have no hold over them.[16] And if Jesus was, as he promised, going to be the one in charge of the Day of Judgement, then he obviously had to rise from the dead first.

Above all, the resurrection fits with the character and nature of Jesus. He was a unique person who had already demonstrated his mastery over death in others; he now displays it in himself. If there is one person in history who could conceivably have risen from the dead, it would surely be Jesus.

ALTERNATIVE EXPLANATIONS

The claims that Jesus rose from the dead cannot simply be dismissed. As with the issue of the deity of Jesus, to simply say that we 'can't believe in the resurrection' or just 'prefer not to believe in it' is not an adequate response. To be intellectually honest, we need to have some alternative explanation that fits the facts.

Such alternatives are hard to find and there are barely a handful of options. Let's briefly consider them.

Jesus didn't die

The issue of the resurrection can be avoided by arguing that Jesus never really died; he simply fainted on the cross and recovered in the tomb. This, of course, requires a succession of improbabilities:

- The Roman soldiers failed to kill Jesus. Given that inflicting death was a key skill for Roman soldiers, this alone would seem remarkable.
- Despite being so weakened by flogging that he couldn't carry the cross beam, Jesus was not killed by the combination of being nailed to a cross, subjected to agony for three hours, having a spear thrust in his side, being covered in spices, wrapped in a shroud and placed in a tomb.
- Neither the soldiers, the watching women, Joseph nor Nicodemus noticed that Jesus was not actually dead.
- Despite being wrapped in grave clothes and covered with spices, Jesus recovered in the tomb and managed to get out of his shroud.
- After having neatly folded up his grave clothes, Jesus managed to push the stone away, escape from the tomb, avoid the guard and, in spite of nail wounds through both heels, walk away.
- Jesus managed to convince his followers that far from being an immediate candidate for an Accident and

Emergency ward, he was actually the risen Lord and the victorious conqueror of death.

- Jesus lied to the disciples about his experience, fooling them into thinking he was raised from the dead.

The resurrection is much easier to believe in.

It was all wishful thinking

Other people hold that the belief in Jesus' resurrection came about through wishful thinking. They believe that after Jesus' death, some sort of tragic desire and longing slowly crystallized into a confident belief that he had been raised from the dead. This flies in the face of many facts:

- There are limits to what wishful thinking can do. We have all experienced things that we wish hadn't happened: tragedies, accidents, mistakes. And we all know that no amount of wishful thinking can undo them. Reality is remarkably immune to the effects of wishful thinking. If wishful thinking was so effective then why aren't there more stories of resurrected martyrs? The hard fact is that we all know that the dead stay dead.
- It completely fails to explain the origin of the church. You don't conjure up the sort of expanding and exciting community that the early Christians had from a crucified and cursed Messiah with nothing more than wishful thinking.

- The time element is too limiting. There is hard evidence that a belief in a resurrected Jesus was the foundation stone of Christianity within twenty years of the crucifixion. There is compelling evidence that it occupied that position in the very earliest Christian beliefs. If the resurrection was wishful thinking, someone in Jerusalem at least would have pointed out the inconvenient fact that Jesus' body was buried in a nearby grave.

The idea that the church and its beliefs were based on a resurrection created by wishful thinking is unbelievable.

It was due to visions

Some alternative explanations for the resurrection appearances attribute them to visions or hallucinations. Yet here again there are problems:

- The psychology of the disciples – defeated, fearful and guilty – is not one that was conducive to receiving visions of a risen and triumphant Lord. In fact, the disciples actually doubted the appearances.
- The resurrection appearances were both unexpected and unimagined.
- The varied nature of the appearances, their extended period, their occurrence to different people in different places, all suggest something other than a 'normal' visionary experience.

- The appearances were clearly solid and physical in nature and very different from visions.
- No amount of vision explains the empty tomb.
- People in Jesus' day were familiar with visions and hallucinations but they were confident this was something very different.

There was a conspiracy

Some people have claimed that Jesus' body was stolen. Here, four things need to be remembered. First, removing the stone would have needed several men, so it couldn't have been a casual thief. Second, the reports that the grave clothes were left neatly behind seem to make any sort of theft improbable. (What sort of thief unwraps a shroud, takes the body away and leaves the grave clothes behind in the tomb?) Third, what about the guard that was there from sometime on Saturday? (Was the body stolen on Friday night and the stone cunningly replaced before the guard arrived? Or was the guard bribed, doped or dodged on the Saturday?) Fourthly, the theft theory merely explains how the tomb came to be empty; it does not explain either the appearances or the extraordinary fact of Christianity.

But if there was a conspiracy, who was responsible for it? In the oldest version of the conspiracy theory, it is the disciples themselves who did it.[17] Such a view raises a vast number of problems. The brutally honest picture of the disciples painted in the gospels suggests that they were so crippled by fear, confusion and guilt that they didn't have the ability or the nerve to steal the body. Besides it is hard to see them committing such a fraudulent act and then, presumably, inventing the accounts of the appearances. And can we really believe the early church, with its reckless dynamism and its vision of reaching the whole world with the good news of Jesus, was built on a foundation of fraud?

Such a resurrection conspiracy by the disciples would have two claims to fame. On the one hand, it would be the most successful hoax ever perpetrated; the secret was kept perfectly and not the faintest echo has come down to us of anyone ever confessing to the theft of Jesus' body. On the other hand, it would be the least profitable hoax ever perpetrated: all except one of the perpetrators were martyred because of it.

So could someone else have stolen the body? Suitable candidates are hard to find. After all, if the body was stolen by Jesus' enemies, why didn't they produce it once the tales of the resurrection started? Why did Paul, once part of the religious leadership, know nothing of it? And why leave the grave clothes behind? And how did anyone conspire to produce the appearances?

There was a mix-up

As an alternative to the theories based on conspiracy we have those based on confusion. Here, the women find the wrong tomb, bump into a Jesus look-alike, mistake gardeners for angels and mishear what is said. And the rest is done by the power of suggestion and that ever-useful standby, wishful thinking.

Yet to explain even the empty tomb as 'History's Greatest Blunder' is incredibly hard. The gospels make it clear the women had been at the tomb on the Friday afternoon, so they knew the place. It would hardly have been a mass graveyard either: given Joseph's status, the tomb would have been in some small garden. And of course, tombs that have empty shrouds in them are a fairly rare occurrence. Finally, again we come across the fact that the Sanhedrin did not display the real tomb with the real body later.

The idea that the belief in the resurrection arose from a mix-up seems hardly adequate to explain even the empty tomb; as an explanation for everything else, it lacks all credibility.

CONCLUSION

If you believe that dead people can *never* rise from the dead then, of course, nothing will convince you that Jesus did rise from the dead. But to take such a view is to be very confident that you know everything about how this still largely unknown universe works. And if you are at all open-minded to the possibility that Jesus might have risen from the dead, then the evidence for the resurrection is very strong.

Yet there is one area of evidence which we have not yet mentioned, an area of evidence for the resurrection of Jesus that can be personally tested. At the heart of the idea of the resurrection is the astounding belief that Jesus himself is alive, that he is not just an historical figure but a present reality: a living person we can communicate with and relate to. The testimony of Christians over the centuries is that this continues to be true: Jesus *is* alive and can be experienced as someone who transforms lives.

Those who truly want to find the risen Jesus, not out of idle curiosity but out of a desire to know him as Saviour, King and Lord of their lives, can still find him.

The Meaning of the Resurrection

The resurrection of Jesus is not just an odd and awesome fact; it is something that overflows with consequences.

The resurrection is a vindication

Imagine a man being punished for what he didn't do. He is publicly humiliated and his reputation, and all he stands for, is dragged into the dirt. If justice is to be done then he must be vindicated: the verdict must be reversed and he must be declared free of guilt. This picture applies to Jesus. The cross saw an innocent Jesus treated as a guilty man, and in the resurrection God is reversing that decision and vindicating him to his followers. By raising Jesus from the dead, God was declaring Jesus innocent and saying in an action what he had said before in words: 'This is my beloved Son, and I am fully pleased with him.'

The resurrection is an authentication

Jesus made extraordinary claims. Those claims require our trust and demand our action. Inevitably, we ask whether he can be trusted. In raising Jesus from the dead, God is authenticating who Jesus is and what he said. The resurrection is God's signature on Jesus' claims. The resurrection says that Jesus can be trusted with our lives.

The resurrection has implications

The implications of Jesus' resurrection are extraordinarily profound and far-reaching: not only are Jesus' claims and teachings authenticated as true and trustworthy but our great enemies of sin, evil and death are defeated. The resurrection shows that God has accepted Jesus' payment for our sin on the cross, that the power of evil has been decisively broken, that our own personal resurrection from the dead is assured. If we believe in the resurrection of Jesus, our attitudes to life, death, the future, *everything*, become altered.

These implications of the resurrection apply not just to our heads but also to our hearts. For the disciples, the resurrection was not simply an historical fact, it was also a personal experience. After Jesus had left them, the two on the road to

Emmaus said to each other 'Didn't our hearts feel strangely warm as he talked with us on the road and explained the Scriptures to us?'[18] Since that day, countless numbers of people have felt their hearts become 'strangely warm' as they have encountered the risen, living Jesus. Indeed, it is that personal experience of the presence of the resurrected Jesus that lies at the very heart of the Christian faith.

To believe in the resurrection of Jesus is not just to put a tick against some box on a list of 'Things I Believe In': it is to let it change how we live.

THE LAST WORD

The portrait of Jesus drawn by the gospels is that of a man of extraordinary power, wisdom and authority. It is a picture of a unique figure unlike anybody before or since, a man who towers above both his own time and all history.

The gospels show a Jesus who is unique in four areas.

Jesus' *teachings* are unique and unparalleled. What he taught was simple, authoritative and of universal significance. His standards for life have never been surpassed. Whenever anyone since has spoken on how we should live, they have done so in the shadow of Jesus' teachings.

Jesus' *claims* about himself are unique. He considered himself God's Son, took God's titles for himself and assumed God's authority. He claimed to be God and his followers believed him.

Jesus' *actions* are unique. He showed an unsurpassed control over the natural and the spiritual world and demonstrated a mastery over people, things and spiritual powers. His actions demonstrated that he had God's power and authority. Jesus' own resurrection – an event whose reality is supported by an extraordinary amount of evidence – is the authentication of all his teaching and the confirmation of all his claims.

Jesus' *character* is unique. Ordinary human beings have weaknesses and are prone to excesses, yet in Jesus we see neither: he is a perfectly balanced human being. In Jesus we see strength without hardness, gentleness without frailty, courage without recklessness and authority without arrogance. In Jesus we see a man whose forgiveness never becomes permissiveness, a man who befriends but who never lets himself be compromised by his friendship, a man of the deepest religious faith who never uses that faith to crush others. When we look at Jesus, we see the human being we were meant to be and the person we so much wish that we were.

Yet for all the remarkable features of Jesus that the gospels paint, what they show is a consistent, credible portrait of a reality, not a fantasy figure. If we are prepared to accept the possibility of a God who could intervene in his own creation, then the picture of Jesus as both perfect Man and God is not just consistent and credible, it is also compelling.

It is not enough, though, simply to sum up who Jesus was, as if he was just another character of history. After all, if we believe in Jesus' resurrection, then he is not just an historical figure: he is still alive and active in the world. In the introduction to Acts, his sequel to his gospel, Luke makes one of the most extraordinary statements ever written: 'In my first book I told you about everything Jesus began to do and teach until the day he ascended to heaven . . . ' In all that he did in his life on earth, says Luke, Jesus was only *beginning* his actions. Those actions continued after his death and they continue today. Whether we find it disturbing or reassuring, the fact that Jesus is alive today is something we have to deal with. You cannot just close the book on Jesus.

Jesus' question to his followers, 'And who do *you* say I am?'[1] still challenges us today. We need to reflect on, and respond to, that question. One seeks in order to understand but one understands in order to seek more.

To choose to follow Jesus is to accept him and all that he is. It is to choose to receive his cleansing from guilt, his guidance, his love and his power to make us into the people we were meant to be. It is to know his presence now and to be given the promise of being eternally with him in heaven.

To choose to follow Jesus is not a trivial decision; it is one that has consequences for every part of our lives. To say 'yes' to Jesus is to accept responsibilities. It is significant that in many of his miracles, Jesus asked for others to help him. Others filled the jars with water at the wedding in Cana, others served the bread and the fish to the five thousand and others rolled the stone away at Lazarus' tomb. Jesus was not a one-man show: where he could, he involved his followers. Ultimately, he left his followers the task of telling the entire world about him. Those who decide to follow Jesus must be prepared for him to give them responsibilities that will stretch them to their limits.

To say 'yes' to Jesus is to be prepared to be challenged. Jesus never disguised the fact that following him was far from easy and he warned that it would involve hardship. In the dark days of 1940, Winston Churchill promised his people in their battle against a powerful enemy 'nothing but blood, toil, tears and sweat'. Jesus' promise to his followers in their battle against a greater darkness is similar. The great difference is that, unlike Churchill, Jesus can guarantee his followers an ultimate victory and an infinite reward. Those who decide to follow Jesus must be prepared to accept hardships as well as responsibilities.

There are only two responses to Jesus: acceptance or rejection. In his time on earth, Jesus never forced himself on anybody and he doesn't do so now; he gives us the right to say 'no' to him. Yet to reject Jesus is the most serious thing any of us can do; it is to reject all the good he offers us now on earth and all that he promises us in heaven.

To accept Jesus, to put following him before everything else, is to have your life transformed permanently. It is to accept his forgiveness, blessing and guidance and, at the same time, to take on willingly whatever responsibility and challenges that he gives.

For all the struggles and pain it may bring, to follow Jesus is to know both an inexpressible joy and an inexhaustible satisfaction.

'Our Father in heaven,
  may your name be honoured.
May your Kingdom come soon.
May your will be done here on earth,
  just as it is in heaven.
Give us our food for today,
  and forgive us our sins, just as we have forgiven those
  who have sinned against us.
And don't let us yield to temptation, but deliver us from
  the evil one.
For yours is the kingdom and the power and the glory.'[3]

FOR FURTHER READING

Books on Jesus

Blomberg, Craig, *Jesus and the Gospels: An Introduction and Survey* (Apollos, 1997)

Bruce, F.F., *The Hard Sayings of Jesus* (Hodder, 1983)

France, R.T., *The Evidence for Jesus* (Hodder, 1999)

Green, Michael, *Who is this Jesus?* (Hodder, 1990)

John, J., *God's Priorities: Living Life from the Lord's Prayer* (Kingsway, 2001)

Stein, Robert, *Jesus the Messiah: A Survey of the Life of Christ* (IVP, 1996)

Wright, N.T., *The Challenge of Jesus* (SPCK, 2000)

Yancey, Philip, *The Jesus I Never Knew* (Marshall Pickering, 1995)

Books on the gospels

Barker, Kenneth, and John Kohlenberger, *The Zondervan NIV Bible Commentary Volume 2: New Testament* (Zondervan, 1994)

Boice, James Montgomery, *Foundations of the Christian Faith* (IVP, 1986)

Drane, John, *Introducing the New Testament* (Lion, 1999)

Keener, Craig S., *The IVP Bible Background Commentary: New Testament* (IVP, 1993)

Wenham, G. J., and others (eds.), *The New Bible Commentary* (IVP, 1994)

See also Tom Wright's series *Matthew For Everyone, Mark For Everyone* etc. (SPCK, 2000)

NOTES

Chapter 1

[1] Jn. 20:4

[2] Jn. 21:11

[3] Josephus, *Antiquities of the Jews* 18.63-64. Translation taken from Bock, Darrell, *Studying the Historical Jesus; a Guide to Sources and Method* (Baker/Apollos, 2002)

Chapter 2

[1] Lk. 1:1–4

[2] Jn. 20:30–31

Chapter 4

[1] Mt. 13:55

[2] Mt. 2:1–12

[3] Josephus; *The Jewish War* 6.9.3. Josephus' figures are generally held to be exaggerated; nevertheless it cannot be doubted that the death toll was appalling.

[4] Jn. 3:1; 7:50–52; 19:39–40

[5] Lk. 6:15

[6] Jn. 7:49

Chapter 5

[1] Lk. 1:13–17, 68–79

[2] Lk. 1:32–33

[3] Lk. 1:35

[4] Mt. 1:18–21

[5] Mt. 1:18–25; Lk. 1:26–35

[6] Lk. 1:35

[7] Mt. 1:22–23

[8] Is. 7:14

[9] Jn. 8:41

[10] Mt. 2:1–12

[11] For example: Mt. 22:30; Mk. 8:38; Lk. 16:22; Jn. 1:51

[12] Jn. 1:1–18

[13] Jn. 1:14

[14] Jn. 1:10–12

Chapter 6

[1] Lk. 3:1–2

[2] Lk. 2:51–52

[3] Mk. 6:3

[4] Mk. 6:3

[5] Heb. 4:15

[6] Josephus, *Antiquities of the Jews* 18.5.2

[7] Mt. 11:7–15

[8] Jn. 1:23

[9] Mk. 11:32

[10] Lk. 3:11–14

[11] Mt. 3:14; Jn. 1:29,33,36

[12] Jn. 1:29–30

[13] Mt. 3:1–2

[14] Mt. 3:13–17; Mk. 1:9–11; Lk. 3:21–22

[15] Mk. 1:9–11

[16] Ps. 2:7

[17] Is. 42:1

[18] Is. 11:2

[19] Acts 1:4–5

[20] Ex. 34:28

[21] Jn. 12:31; 14:30; 16:11

[22] Mt. 6:13; 13:19

[23] Jn. 8:44

[24] Jn. 8:44

[25] Mt. 13:24–30, 36–43

[26] Jn. 12:31

[27] i.e. 1 Cor. 10:13; 2 Cor. 11:14; Jas. 4:7; 1 Pet. 5:8; 1 Jn. 4:4

[28] Col. 2:15; Heb. 2:14; Rev. 20:10

[29] Mt. 4:3

[30] Deut. 8:3

[31] Mt. 4:5–6

[32] Mt. 4:7

[33] Deut. 6:16

[34] Mt. 4:8–9

[35] Mt. 4:10

[36] Lk. 4:13

Chapter 7

1. Lk. 3:1–3,23
2. See Jn. 1:35–50
3. Mk. 3:7–8
4. Mk. 1:15
5. Mt. 14:13–21; Mk. 6:30–44; Lk. 9:11–17; Jn. 6:5–13
6. Jn. 6:14–15
7. Mk. 6:45–46; Jn. 6:15
8. Mk. 1:40–45; 5:43
9. Mt. 15:1–20; Mk. 7:1–23
10. Mk. 8:27
11. Mt. 16:13–20; see also Mk. 8:27–30; Lk. 9:18–20
12. Mk. 8:31; see also Mt. 16:21; Lk. 9:22
13. Mt. 16:22
14. Mt. 16:24; see also Lk. 14:27
15. Mt. 17:1–13; Mk. 9.2–13; Lk. 9.28–36; see also the reference in 2 Pet. 1:16–18
16. Mt. 17:2
17. Lk. 9:30–31
18. Mt. 17:5
19. Ex. 19:1, 24
20. Ex. 24:15–18; 1 Kgs. 8:10–11; 2 Chr. 5:13–14; Ps. 97:2
21. 2 Pet. 1:16–18
22. Mk. 9:30–32
23. Mt. 17:22–23; Mk. 9:31–32; Lk. 9:43–45
24. Jn. 10:22–40
25. Mk. 10:1,10; Jn. 10:40
26. Mt. 27:55; Lk. 23:49
27. Mt. 20:17–19; Mk. 10:32–34; Lk. 18:31–34

28 Mk. 11:11–12; Jn. 11:1

29 Mt. 11:18–19

30 Mk. 2:22

31 Lk. 4:14–30

32 *The Jewish War* 6.9.3

33 Mt. 12:24

34 Jn. 11:1–44

35 Jn. 11:45–53

36 Jn. 11:54

37 Jn. 12:9–11

38 Matthew, Mark and John all describe what was clearly the same event (Mt. 26:6–13, Mk. 14:3–9 and Jn. 12:1–11). Although the impression gained from Matthew and Mark is that the meal occurred in the Last Week itself, John is the only one who gives it a specific time, placing it just before the entry into Jerusalem.

Chapter 8

1 Mk. 1:16–20; Mt. 9:9

2 Mk. 3:13–15

3 Mk. 3:13–14

4 Is. 11:10–16; 49:6–12; 56:8; Micah 2:12–13

5 Acts 1:21

6 Mk. 10:13; 11:1–3; Jn. 4:8

7 Mt. 28:10; Jn. 20:17

8 Mt. 10:1–4; Mk. 3:13–19; Lk. 6:13–16; Acts 1:13

9 Mk.1:30; 1 Cor. 9:5

10 Mk. 3:17

11 Jn. 20:24–25

12 Jn. 11:16; 20:28

13 Mt. 27:56; Mk. 15:40; 16:1; Lk. 24:10
14 See Acts 4:13
15 Acts 12:2
16 Lk. 10:1–20; see also Jn. 6:60–66
17 Lk. 9:57–58
18 Lk. 8:1–3
19 Lk. 18:35–19:10; see Mk. 10:46–52
20 Hanson, K.C., and D. E. Oakman, *Palestine in the Time of Jesus: Social Structures and Social Conflicts* (Fortress Press, 1998) page 14
21 Jn. 19:38
22 Lk. 24:1–11, 13–35; 1 Cor. 15:6
23 *Against Apion* 2:25
24 Jn. 4:27
25 Jn. 20:11–18
26 Lk. 10:39; see Acts 22.3
27 Jn. 8:1–11
28 Mt. 5:27–28
29 Lk. 15:8–10
30 Jn. 4:1–26, 39–42
31 Josephus, *Life*, 76
32 Mk. 10:11

Chapter 9

1 Mt. 9:27–31; Mk. 8:22–26
2 Lk. 5:12–14
3 Jn. 5:1–15
4 Mk. 1:29–31; Jn. 4:43–53
5 Lk. 22:50–51
6 Mk. 5:24–34

[7] Mk. 3:1–5

[8] Mk. 5:35–43; Lk. 7:11–17; Jn. 11:1–44

[9] Mt. 14:15–21; 15:32–38; Mk. 6:35–44; 8:1–9

[10] Jn. 2:1–11

[11] Mt. 8:23–27; Mk. 4:37–41

[12] Mt. 14:25; Mk. 6:48–51

[13] Lk. 5:4–11; Jn. 21:1–11

[14] i.e. Jn. 1:47–49; 2:24–25

[15] Mt. 10:8; Mk. 1:21–27; 6:13; Lk. 13:32

[16] Mt. 8:4; Mk. 5:40, 43; 7:33, 36

[17] Mt. 9:29; Mk. 1:31,41; 5:41

[18] Mt. 16:1–4; Lk. 11:29–30

[19] Mt. 26:51–59; 27:39–44

[20] Mt. 14:14; 15:32; 20:34; Mk. 1:41

[21] Mt. 14:13–21; Mk. 6:32–44; Lk. 9:10–17; Jn. 6:1–15

[22] Acts 2:22

[23] As in Josephus, *Antiquities of the Jews* 18.63f. Although the passage may have been altered, the reference to Jesus doing amazing deeds is thought to be original. Suggestions that Jesus' miracles were due to black magic can be found in the Babylonian Talmud (*Sanhedrin 43a*) and are attributed to a Jew, Trypho, in Justin Martyr's Dialogue with Trypho 69.7 and a Greek, Celsus, in Origen's *Contra Celsum* 1.6.

[24] There is an interesting article ('Why doctors now believe faith heals') in the September 2002 *Reader's Digest*.

[25] An excellent and unsensational resource on matters to do with prayer and healing (and much else) is to be found on the website of the Christian Medical Fellowship (*www.cmf.org*), an organization which has a membership of over five thousand doctors.

[26] Jn. 1:1–14

27 Ex. 16:14–35; Mk. 6:30–44

28 1 Kgs. 17:17–23; Lk. 7:11–16

29 2 Kgs. 5; Lk. 17:11–19

30 Lk. 24:19

31 Jn. 3:2; Acts 10:38

32 Mt. 11:4–5; see also Mt. 8:16–17 (compare Is. 35:5; 53:4; 61:1)

33 Mk. 4:41

34 Ps. 32; 65:7; 107:23–32

35 Mt. 14:25–33; see Job 9:8

36 Mk. 2:9–11

37 Mt. 9:32–34; 12:22; Mk. 1:21–28; 5:1–20; 7:24–30; 9:14–29

38 Lk. 11:20

39 Mk. 3:26–27

40 Mt. 8:11; Rev. 21:4

41 Lk. 22:50–51

42 Ex. 34:6; Ps. 116:5; Mt. 9:36; 14:14

43 Jn. 20:30–31

44 Mt. 12:24; Mk. 3:22

45 Mt. 11:21

Chapter 10

1 Mt. 10:24–25; 26:18

2 Jn. 7:45–46

3 Lk. 13:1–3; 18:15–17

4 Mt. 7:12

5 Mk. 7:15

6 Mk. 2:27

7 Lk. 12:15

8 Mt. 5:3–4

9   Mt. 10:38–39
10 Lk. 22:26
11 Mt. 22:20–22
12 Mk. 4:30–32
13 Ezek. 17:23; 31:6; Dan. 4:9–22
14 Lk. 18:9–14
15 Lk. 15
16 Lk. 15:1–2
17 Lk. 15:11–32
18 Mt. 13:10
19 Mk. 4:33–34
20 Mt. 7:28–29
21 Mt. 9:36 NIV
22 Mk. 10:21; Jn. 11:5
23 Mk. 3:1–6
24 Mk. 11:15–17
25 Mk. 10:14
26 Mt. 23:13–36

Chapter 11

1   Mk. 1:14–15; see also Lk. 4:43
2   Dan. 2:44
3   Lk. 17:21; Mt. 12:28
4   Lk. 13:20–21
5   Mk. 4:26–29
6   Mt. 24:14; Lk. 13:29
7   Mt. 12:28; Lk. 11:20
8   Mt. 13:24–30, 36–43
9   Mt. 25:1–13

[10]   Mt. 19:28; 25:31–46

[11]   Mt. 13:36–43, 49–51; Mk. 9:47–48

[12]   Lk. 20:34–38

[13]   Mt. 8:11; 22:1–14; 24:14; 25:1–13; Lk. 14:16–24

[14]   Lk. 13:22–27

[15]   See Lk. 18:25–30. Here Jesus says how hard it is for a rich man to enter the Kingdom of God and the disciples reply 'Who then can be saved?' In the next few verses the Kingdom is linked with 'eternal life'. In Mt. 7:13–14 the 'Kingdom' and 'life' are clearly the same.

[16]   Mt. 13:45–46; the parable of the hidden treasure (Mt. 13:44) makes the same point.

[17]   Mk. 8:36

[18]   Mt. 13:42; 25:30,46

[19]   Mt. 20:1–16; Mk. 10:15

[20]   Lk. 12:32

[21]   Mt. 7:13–14

[22]   Lk. 18:16–17

[23]   Lk. 23:42–43

[24]   Mk. 1:15

[25]   Mt. 11:28–30

[26]   Mt. 7:21–23; Mk. 4:1–20

[27]   Mt. 16:24; 19:12; Mk. 10:21–27; Lk. 9:57–62

[28]   Jn. 3:3,5

[29]   Mk. 2:21–22

[30]   Mk. 14:36

[31]   Rom. 8:15; Gal. 4:5–6

[32]   Mt. 6:9–13

[33]   Mt. 5–7. The title 'The Sermon on the Mount' comes from Mt. 5:1, where we read that Jesus went up on the mountainside to teach.

34 Mt. 5:21–22

35 Mt. 5:27–28

36 Mt. 12:33–35

37 Mt. 7:17–18

38 Mt. 15:1–20

39 Lk. 10:25–37

40 Mt. 22:37–40

41 Jn. 15:4

42 Lk. 11:13; 24:49; see Acts 1:8

43 Mt. 5:33–37

44 Mt. 23:1–35

45 Mt. 6:9–13; Lk. 11:5–13; 18:1–8

46 Mt. 6:6-8; 7:7–11; Mk. 11:22–25

47 Mt. 6:12,14,15; 18:21–35

48 Mt. 5:38–42

49 Mt. 7:1–5

50 Lk. 22:25–27

51 Mt. 6:19–34; Lk. 12:33–34

52 Jn. 13:34–35

53 Mt. 6:25–34

54 Mt. 6:10

55 Mt. 5:3–10. These are traditionally called 'The Beatitudes', from the Latin word *beatus*; 'blessed'

Chapter 12

1 The idea that Jesus saves people is a major theme in Luke, e.g. 1:68–79; 2:11; 2:30–32; 5:29–32; 10:29–37; 19:1–10; 23:43

2 Mt. 1:21

3 Lk. 2:11

4 Lk. 4:18–19: Jesus is quoting Is. 61:1–2

5 Mt. 9:36 NIV

6 Mt. 11:28–30

7 Jn. 6:35; 8:12; 10:7,9; 10:11; 11:25; 14:6; 15:5

8 Mk. 10:45

9 Is. 42:1–4; 49:1–7; 50:4–9; 52:13–53:12. The last passage is the one most commonly referred to in the New Testament.

10 Jn. 10:11

11 Jn. 1:29

12 Mt. 16:16,20

13 Mt. 9:27; 15:22; Mk. 10:47–48

14 Mk. 12:6

15 2 Sam. 7:14; Ps. 2:7–12

16 Jn. 10:30; 14:9

17 Mt. 11:27

18 Mt. 3:17; 17:5

19 Jn. 20:17

20 Jn. 3:16

21 Dan. 7:13–14

22 Mk. 14:62

23 Mk. 11:3

24 Acts 2:36

25 Rom. 10:9; Phil. 2:11

26 Jn. 20:28

27 Jn. 6:35; 8:12; 10:7,11; 11:25; 14:6; 15:1

28 Jn. 8:58 (NIV)

29 Ex. 3:14

30 Lk. 22:20

31 Mt. 7:24

[32] Mk. 2:5–7

[33] Mt. 5:31–32, 38–39

[34] Mk. 7:1–23

[35] Mt. 12:38–42; Jn. 4:12; 8:53,56

[36] Mt. 11:11

[37] Mt. 12:6

[38] Jn. 2:18–21

[39] Mt. 12:8

[40] Mk. 13:31

[41] Mt. 11:27; 28:18–20

[42] Mt. 10:32–33; 11:6; 25:31–46; Mk. 8:34–38

[43] Mt. 7:22–23; 25:31–46

[44] Lk. 14:26

[45] Jn. 14:13–14; 16:23–24

[46] Mk. 5:34; 10:52; Lk. 7:50; 17:19

[47] Mt. 10:40; Mk. 9:37

[48] Jn. 3:13; 17:5,24

[49] Jn. 8:58

[50] Jn. 6:62; 16:28

[51] Mt. 28:20

[52] Jn. 1:1–14

[53] Mt. 28:18–20

[54] See, for example, Phil. 2:6–11; Col. 1:15–20; Heb. 1:1–3

[55] Jn. 4:6

[56] Mt. 4:2

[57] Jn. 19:28

[58] Mt. 26:53

[59] Mt. 12:25; Jn. 1:48; 2:24; 16:30

[60] Mt. 24:36

[61] Lk. 2:52

Chapter 13

[1] Mt. 21:1–11; Mk. 11:1–11; Lk. 19:28–40; Jn.12:12–19
[2] Mk. 11:9–10
[3] Jn. 12:13
[4] 1 Macc. 13:51; see also 2 Macc. 10:7
[5] Zech. 9:9
[6] Mt. 21:18–22; Mk. 11:12–14, 20–24
[7] Mt. 21:12–13; Mk. 11:15–17; Lk. 19:45–46
[8] Is. 56:7–8; Jer. 7:1–15
[9] Mt. 21:23–25:46; Mk. 11:27–13:37; Lk. 20:1–21:38
[10] Mk. 11:27
[11] Mt. 21:28–32, 33–46; 22:1–14; Mk. 12:1–12; Lk. 20:9–19
[12] Mt. 24:1–51; Mk. 13:1–37; Lk. 21:5–36
[13] Mt. 24:2
[14] Mt. 24:3 NIV
[15] Mt. 24:36
[16] Mk. 14:1
[17] Deut. 21:22–23
[18] Mt. 26:14–16; Mk. 14:10–11
[19] Mt. 26:20–29; Mk. 14:17–25; Lk. 22:14–20; see also 1 Cor. 11:17–34
[20] Lk. 22:24
[21] Jn. 13:3–17
[22] Ex. 24:8
[23] Ex. 24:9–11
[24] Jer. 31:31–34
[25] Lk. 22:19
[26] Jn. 13:18–29

27 Jn. 14-16

28 Jn. 17

29 Mt. 26:36–46; Mk. 14:32–42; Lk. 22:39–46; Jn. 18:1–9

30 Mt. 26:37–38; Mk. 14:33–34; Lk. 22:44

31 Mk. 14:35–36

32 Gal. 3:13

Chapter 14

1 Mt. 26:47–56; Mk. 14:43–52; Lk. 22:47–53; Jn. 18:1–9

2 Mt. 26:57–27:31; Mk. 14:53–15:20; Lk. 22:54–23:25; Jn. 18:12–19:16

3 Josephus, *Antiquities* 20.198; Jn. 18:19–24

4 Mt. 26:57–68; Mk. 14:53–65; Lk. 22:66–71

5 Mt. 26:63

6 Mt. 26:64

7 Mt. 26:65

8 Dan. 7:13

9 Jn. 18:15–18

10 Lk. 23:8–12

11 Mk. 15:7; Lk. 23:18–19

12 Josephus, *Jewish War* 2:21,5

13 Jn. 19:6

14 Jn. 19:7

15 Jn. 19:12

16 Jn. 19:15 NIV

17 *Antiquities* 18:63–64

18 Jn. 11:48

19 Acts 4:27

20 Mt. 27:31–56; Mk. 15:21–41; Lk. 23:26–49; Jn. 19:17–33

21 *Declamationes minores* 274

22 Mk. 15:21

23 Mt. 27:38–44; Mk. 15:16–20, 29–32; Lk. 23:35–36

24 Is. 52:14

25 Is. 53:3

26 Is. 53:4–5

27 Is. 53:7-8

28 Is. 53:12

29 Jn. 19:27

30 Joel 2:2; Amos 8:9

31 2 Cor. 5:21

32 Jn. 1:29

33 See Jn. 17:4

34 Jn. 19:34

35 Mt. 27:51; Mk. 15:38; Lk. 23:45

36 Mt. 27:54; Mk. 15:39; Lk. 23:47

37 Mt. 27:57,59; Mk. 15:43,45; Lk. 23:50–52; Jn. 19:38

38 Mt. 27:62–64

39 Mt. 27:65–66

40 Mt. 27:42

41 Jn. 1:4

Chapter 15

1 1 Cor. 15:14,17

2 1 Cor. 15:3–8

3 Gal. 1:18

4 Mt. 28:1–10; Mk. 16:1–8; Lk. 24:1–12; Jn. 20:1–10

5 Jn. 20:5–7

6 Lk. 24:42–43

7   Mt. 28:18–20

8   Compare Mk. 3:21 and Jn. 7:5 with Acts 12:17, Gal. 1:19; 2:9

9   1 Cor. 15:20,49

10   Jn. 20:1–10

11   Jn. 20:17

12   Lk. 24:25, 37–38

13   Acts 1:22; 2:24,32; 3:15

14   Baba Kamma 88a: see also Josephus, *Antiquities* 4:8.15

15   Acts 8:1–3

16   Acts 2:24

17   Mt. 28:13–15

18   Lk. 24:32

Chapter 16

1   Mt. 16:15

2   Mt. 6:9–13